INTRODUCTION AND CONTENTS

Welcome!

This guidebook will walk you through the *5 Money Personalities* DVD-based study. As you work through each of the twelve weekly sessions, you'll find yourself discovering new ways to think about your money and your relationship.

Here's how to make the most of this series:

1. As you watch each of the weekly DVDs, follow along in your guidebook, answering the questions as you go.

2. **Interactive Discussion Points**—each session includes interactive questions designed for you and your spouse or group to discuss.

3. **Weekly Activities**—these are designed to give you short activities to do throughout the week to drive home the points of the session. For the first four days you do your activity on your own; then on the fifth day take some time to reflect on your week together.

Have fun, stay engaged, and connect like you never have before.

Make It Happen,
The Money Couple

Scott and Bethany Plamer
www.TheMoneyCouple.com

The **5** Money Personalities™ Guidebook

Scott and Bethany Palmer
THE MONEY COUPLE®

THOMAS NELSON
Since 1798

NASHVILLE   DALLAS   MEXICO CITY   RIO DE JANEIRO

Published in Nashville, Tennessee, by Thomas Nelson. Thomas Nelson is a registered trademark of Thomas Nelson, Inc.

Thomas Nelson, Inc., titles may be purchased in bulk for educational, business, fund-raising, or sales promotional use. For information, please e-mail SpecialMarkets@ThomasNelson.com.

Unless otherwise noted, all Scripture quotations are taken from the Holy Bible, New International Version®, NIV®. Copyright © 1973, 1978, 1984, 2011 by Biblica, Inc.™ Used by permission of Zondervan. All rights reserved worldwide. www.zondervan.com

Scripture quotations marked (NKJV) are from THE NEW KING JAMES VERSION. © 1982 by Thomas Nelson, Inc. Used by permission. All rights reserved.

Scripture quotations marked (NLT) are from the Holy Bible, New Living Translation. © 1996. Used by permission of Tyndale House Publishers, Inc., Wheaton, Illinois 60189. All rights reserved.

ISBN: 9-781-4016-7833-3

TABLE OF **CONTENTS**

Session 1

Your Money Relationship

So encourage each other and build each other up, just as you are already doing.

—1 Thessalonians 5:11 (NLT)

It all starts with the vows: For richer or poorer. We stand up at our weddings and recite those vows fully expecting that we will happily stand by each other, no matter what. We have big dreams about the life we're starting with this person we love so much.

And then life happens. It doesn't matter if things go along just as you planned or if your plans get derailed early on. The bottom line is that life, no matter how great it is, pushes a lot of your hopes and dreams to the side. You have jobs. You have kids. You buy a house. You lose a house. Your parents get older. You find yourselves stressed out by the present and worried about the future. And over time, through no fault of your own, those dreams you had for your life together get put on the back burner and one by one, they start to dry up and disappear.

If you think about the dreams you had when you got married, most of them have some kind of money component—buying a house, having children, getting a job, moving to a new city, traveling, spending time with friends. Money doesn't equal happiness, but money does play a part in whether our dreams turn into reality.

There's a reason we take vows to stick together in richer or poorer. Money ripples into every part of our lives as couples. That's why, whether you have it or you don't, money can test a relationship.

Because money trickles out of and into just about every decision we make during the day, it's not surprising that couples clash over money. It's like a constant pop quiz, one you're bound to fail unless you and your spouse have a strong Money Relationship.

Your Money Relationship is not the same thing as your financial arrangement. Your financial plans, your debt, your investments, your taxes, your budget—those make up one aspect of your life together. And that's not what this book is about. We want to focus on the relationship *behind* that part of your life, your Money Relationship. That's the part of your marriage that involves all of those little, day-to-day decisions about money.

You and your spouse started your lives together with big dreams. So now it's time to do what it takes to reclaim those dreams, to quit arguing about money and heal your Money Relationship.

1. What percentage of relationships end over money?[1] _____

2. A Money Relationship is the decisions couples make where _____ is involved.

---

1. "Expert Advice: Love by the Numbers; Your new marriage is bliss—until the bickering over finances begins. How to keep money from wrecking your home life," [U.S. Edition Edition] Raina Kelley. *Newsweek*. New York: Apr 9, 2007. Vol. 149, Iss. 14; p. 48.

3. A Money Relationship is NOT:

- _____

- _____

- _____

4. A Money Relationship IS:

- _____

- _____

- _____

5. You are learning how to bring _____ and _____ together.

Notes:

_____

_____

_____

_____

_____

_____

_____

_____

_____

_____

_____

_____

_____

INTERACTIVE DISCUSSION POINTS

1. What are your expectations for the next 90 days?

   _____

   _____

2. List one or two decisions you have made recently that involve money.

   _____   _____

3. List ten decisions you made in the last week that involved money.

   _____   _____

   _____   _____

   _____   _____

   _____   _____

   _____   _____

4. Now list one or two decisions that you didn't think of as money decisions at the time, but that you now realize had a money component.

   _____   _____

5. First Thessalonians 5:11 tells us to encourage and build each other up. Take a moment to tell your partner how you would like to encourage him or her over the next twelve weeks.

WEEKLY ACTIVITY

For the next few days, write down one decision each day that involved money.

Day 1: _____

Day 2: _____

Day 3: _____

Day 4: _____

Day 5: Come together: Share your lists. Are you surprised by how often you make money decisions?

_____

_____

_____

_____

_____

_____

_____

Session 2

Getting to Know ME

For you created my inmost being; you knit me together in my mother's womb. I praise you because I am fearfully and wonderfully made; your works are wonderful, I know that full well.

—Psalm 139:13–14

Everyone thinks about and deals with money in a unique, highly personal way. That's because each of us has something we call a *Money Personality* and there are five of them. Each of the five Money Personalities has its strengths and its challenges. Each of them can help you make great financial decisions and each of them has the potential to get you into financial trouble. That's why we remind people that there is no right or wrong Money Personality. They are what they are.

The goal in discovering your Money Personality isn't to point out your flaws. It's to help you understand yourself and the way you think about and deal with money because the more you know about yourself and your perspective on money, the better equipped you are to work with your spouse to build a strong Money Relationship.

Your Money Personality is the lens through which you make money decisions. It's what motivates you to wait until that sweater is on sale. It's what drives you to put 30 percent of your paycheck in your savings account. It's what makes you treat everyone to dinner when you're out with friends. And since money touches every decision you make, your Money Personality frames your perspective on life.

Your Money Personality isn't a separate piece of you—it's fully integrated into other parts of your personality and vice versa. The deeper your recognition of the ways your Money Personality influences your life and your decisions, the more prepared you are to dig into your Money Relationship and make it stronger.

1. There is no right Money Personality and no _____ Money Personality.

2. Everyone has _____ of the _____ Money Personalities.

3. Everyone has a Primary and a _____ Money Personality.

4. The five Money Personalities are:

   #1 _____

   #2 _____

   #3 _____

   #4 _____

   #5 _____

Notes:

_____

_____

_____

_____

_____

_____

_____

_____

_____

_____

INTERACTIVE DISCUSSION POINTS

1. Based on the information from the DVD session, identify your Primary and Secondary Money Personality:

   Primary _____

   Secondary _____

2. List a few reasons those Money Personalities seem to fit you. Be sure to include both your Primary and Secondary Money Personalities.

   _____

   _____

   _____

3. How do you see these Money Personalities play out in other people you know?

_____

_____

_____

_____

_____

WEEKLY ACTIVITY

This week you'll be digging in to your Money Personality so you have a better sense of how you think about money.

Day 1: Go to www.TheMoneyCouple.com and take the Money Personality Profile.

My Primary Money Personality is _____

My Secondary Money Personality is _____

Day 2: Today I noticed my Primary Money Personality when I:

_____

_____

_____

Day 3: Today I noticed my Secondary Money Personality when I:

_____

_____

_____

Day 4: Answer the following questions:

I like my Primary and Secondary Money Personalities because:

_____

_____

_____

My Primary and Secondary Money Personalities can be a challenge because:

_____

_____

_____

Day 5: Come together: Describe your Money Personality to your partner. Give specific examples of how your Money Personalities drove decisions you made this week.

_____

_____

_____

_____

_____

_____

_____

_____

Session 3

The Opposite Dynamic

It is for freedom that Christ has set us free.
Stand firm, then, and do not let yourselves
be burdened again by a yoke of slavery.

—Galatians 5:1

Once you know your Primary and Secondary Money Personality, you'll start noticing them playing out in all kinds of ways. If you're a Risk Taker, for example, you'll start to notice the little decisions you make every day that have an element of the unknown to them—checking out a new restaurant, pursuing a new business contact, trying a new recipe. If you're a Saver, you'll notice that you compare prices at the grocery store, or automatically head to the clearance rack when you're shopping.

But that's just your Primary Money Personality at work. Your Secondary Money Personality, while not as prominent as your Primary Money Personality, still impacts the way you view money. That's why there are Spenders who experience serious buyer's remorse and Flyers who retire as millionaires.

We've learned that there are certain combinations of Primary and Secondary Money Personalities that create something we call the *Opposite Dynamic*. The Opposite Dynamic is the internal conflict so many of us experience when our Primary and Secondary Money Personalities clash.

The Opposite Dynamic is the result of your Money Personalities having competing needs. That competition creates internal tension. And that tension can quickly creep into your Money Relationship. So we're going to take some time to break down this idea of the Opposite Dynamic so you can see how that internal tension might be seeping into your marriage.

1. Understanding who we are brings added _____ to the relationship.

2. We are going to look at what we call the
"_____ _____."

3. On the left side of the spectrum there are two Money Personalities:

   _____

   _____

4. On the right side of the spectrum there are three Money Personalities:

   _____

   _____

   _____

5. If your Primary and Secondary Money Personalities are on the opposite side of the spectrum you have an
"_____ _____."

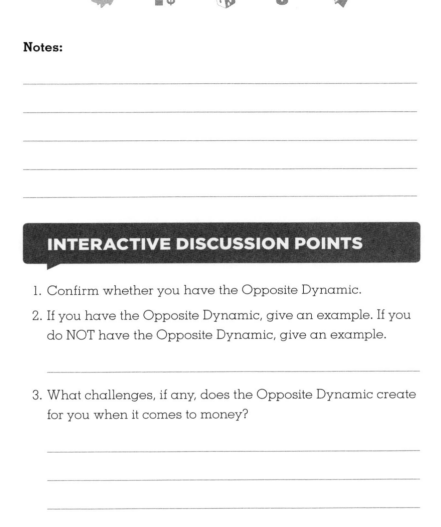

Notes:

_____

_____

_____

_____

_____

INTERACTIVE DISCUSSION POINTS

1. Confirm whether you have the Opposite Dynamic.

2. If you have the Opposite Dynamic, give an example. If you do NOT have the Opposite Dynamic, give an example.

_____

3. What challenges, if any, does the Opposite Dynamic create for you when it comes to money?

_____

_____

_____

WEEKLY ACTIVITY

If you do have the Opposite Dynamic: For the next four days, write down examples of how this dynamic shows up in your money decisions.

If you don't have the Opposite Dynamic: For the next four days, write down examples of how not having this dynamic shows up in your money decisions.

Day 1: _____

Day 2: _____

Day 3: _____

Day 4: _____

Day 5: Come together: Share your examples from the week.

_____

_____

_____

_____

_____

_____

_____

Session 4

The Big Reveal

The LORD God said, "It is not good for the man to be alone. I will make a helper suitable for him."
—Genesis 2:18

Knowing your Money Personality gives you huge insight into why you think the way you do about money. Knowing your spouse's Money Personality gives you huge insight into your spouse. And isn't that what makes relationships hum? Knowing each other, really getting what makes the other person tick?

That's why there's more to your Money Relationship than your financial plans. Every time you make a decision, you're bringing your perspective on life to the table. And nothing feels better than making decisions with someone who understands and respects your perspective.

If you've ever traveled someplace where they didn't speak the same language as you, you know how frustrating it can be to try to bridge the language barrier. But when you finally find someone who speaks your language, it's such a relief! You feel heard and understood.

The same thing happens when you and your spouse understand each other's Money Personalities. It's like you've learned how to speak the same language. And speaking your spouse's language is a great way to demonstrate your love and respect.

For so many couples, their Money Relationship is a tangle of false assumptions, old resentments, and constant blame. At the root of all of that is a misunderstanding of who the other person is and why he or she behaves a certain way. But when these couples discover their Money Personalities and take the time to really understand each other, they begin to see past those assumptions and resentments.

1. It is crucial to _____ and _____ your Money Personalities.

2. I am going to get to know my spouse's Money Personalities through The Big _____.

3. The greatest number of Money Personalities we could have in our relationship is _____.

Notes:

_____

_____

_____

_____

_____

_____

_____

_____

INTERACTIVE DISCUSSION POINTS

1. Write down your spouse's Money Personalities:

Primary _____

Secondary _____

2. Map your Big Reveal:

	My Name	Spouse's Name
Primary		
Secondary		

3. I am *not* surprised about our Big Reveal because:

_____

_____

_____

4. I am surprised about our Big Reveal because:

_____

_____

_____

5. How can God use your Money Personalities to strengthen your relationship?

_____

_____

_____

_____

WEEKLY ACTIVITY

Day 1: List five examples of positive attributes of your spouse's *Primary* Money Personality:

_____

_____

_____

_____

_____

Day 2: List five examples of positive attributes of your spouse's *Secondary* Money Personality:

_____

_____

_____

_____

_____

Day 3: Write down one example of a challenging attribute of your spouse's *Primary and Secondary* Money Personalities:

_____

_____

Day 4: Complete these sentences.

I appreciate my spouse's Money Personality because:

_____

_____

_____

I would appreciate my spouse acknowledging the following attribute of my *Primary* Money Personality:

_____

I would appreciate my spouse acknowledging the following attribute of my *Secondary* Money Personality:

_____

Day 5: Come together:

    a. Tell your spouse five attributes of his or her Money Personalities.

    b. Show appreciation of your spouse's Money Personalities by giving examples of how his or her Money Personalities help you as a person and as a couple.

_____

_____

_____

    c. Say to each other, "I would feel appreciated if you acknowledged _____ in regard to my Money Personalities."

Session 5

Opposites Attract

As iron sharpens iron, so one person sharpens another.

—Proverbs 27:17 (UPDATED NIV)

We have found that roughly 90 percent of the people we work with have the Opposite Dynamic in their relationship. That doesn't surprise us a bit. There's something subconscious in the way we are drawn to the opposite Money Personality. We recognize that this other person will add something important to our lives. A Security Seeker might be drawn to the Risk Taker because the Risk Taker brings the thrill of the unknown into the Security Seeker's predictable life. A Spender might be drawn to a Saver's sense of responsibility and stability. A Saver might be drawn to a Flyer's generosity. Whatever it is, it seems that when it comes to Money Personalities, the old adage is right: opposites attract.

A strong marriage is only possible when couples reclaim that attraction, when they stop seeing the downsides of their differences and start loving the way they complement each other. But that can't happen until you take an honest look at how your Money Personalities impact your Money Relationship.

Many of us have the Opposite Dynamic in ourselves. Our primary Money Personality is on one side of the scale and our secondary Money Personality is on the other side. The same thing happens in couples. The vast majority of the couples we work with have the Opposite Dynamic in their relationship. And it's often that Opposite Dynamic that causes conflict.

If you're willing to shift your perspective and see your partner's Money Personality as an asset in your Money Relationship, you'll find yourselves moving forward with the belief that you are stronger together than you can ever be on your own.

1. Earn a _____ on your spouse.

2. Let's review the Opposite Dynamic:

On the left side of the spectrum there are two Money Personalities:

_____

_____

On the right side of the spectrum there are three Money Personalities:

_____

_____

_____

3. Ann and Joe are like _____% of the population who have the Opposite Dynamic either between their own Money Personalities or in their relationship.

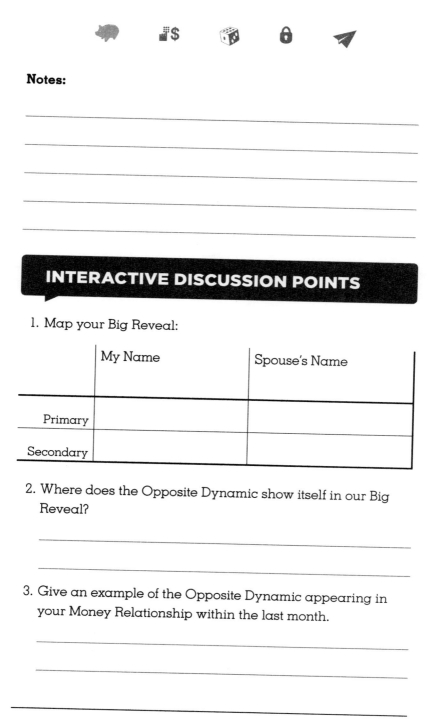

Notes:

_____

_____

_____

_____

_____

INTERACTIVE DISCUSSION POINTS

1. Map your Big Reveal:

	My Name	Spouse's Name
Primary		
Secondary		

2. Where does the Opposite Dynamic show itself in our Big Reveal?

_____

_____

3. Give an example of the Opposite Dynamic appearing in your Money Relationship within the last month.

_____

_____

4. How can God use your Opposite Dynamic to strengthen your marriage?

_____

_____

_____

WEEKLY ACTIVITY

For the next four days, write down examples of how the Opposite Dynamic plays out in your relationship.

Day 1: _____

Day 2: _____

Day 3: _____

Day 4: _____

Day 5: Come together: Share your examples from the week.

_____

_____

_____

_____

_____

_____

_____

Session 6

Your Money or Your Wife

You shall not bear false witness against your neighbor.
—Exodus 20:16 (NKJV)

We use the term *financial infidelity* to refer to a host of money-related behaviors: lying about money, hiding money, secretly hoarding money, controlling money, or anything that involves one spouse being less-than-honest with the other.

Financial infidelity, like sexual infidelity, usually starts out with a small breach of trust. You say you're going to spend $100 and you spend $200. You hang on to a credit card that's in your name "just in case" and never tell your spouse you're still using it. You keep a little secret stash of cash in your underwear drawer, a stash that goes from $50 to $100 to $500 to $5000, and you never tell your spouse about it.

But some financial infidelity, the kind that does the most damage in a relationship, is meant to be hurtful. It's the secret credit cards, the intentional lies about spending, the total control over the finances, the hidden accounts. That's the stuff that pushes marriages to the brink of divorce—and beyond.

The emotional toll of financial infidelity is far more devastating than the toll it takes on your money. You can figure out how to recover from overspending. You can find a way to get some money put away for retirement. You can work through almost any money problem. But it takes a whole other kind of repair work to recover from the loss of trust that comes from financial infidelity.

There's a little financial infidelity in every relationship. But before you can put an end to it, you need to know how it's worked its way into your Money Relationship.

1. Financial infidelity definition:
   The act of lying about, _____, or secretly hoarding money in a relationship.

2. _____ secrets really hurt!

3. _____% of women have a secret account or stash of cash.

Notes:

_____

_____

_____

_____

_____

INTERACTIVE DISCUSSION POINTS

1. What is the craziest financial infidelity story you have ever heard?

_____

_____

2. Why do you think couples struggle with financial infidelity?

_____

_____

3. How does financial infidelity hurt a relationship?

_____

_____

WEEKLY ACTIVITY

For the next four days, notice examples of financial infidelity you see around you: a friend who makes a purchase even though she knows her spouse wouldn't like it, a TV show where a character lies about finances, a news story about credit card debt run amok.

Day 1: _____

Day 2: _____

Day 3: _____

Day 4: _____

Day 5: Come together: What was the most surprising example of financial infidelity you found this week?

_____

_____

_____

_____

_____

_____

Session 7

Get to the Root

Do nothing out of selfish ambition or vain conceit, but in humility consider others better than yourselves. Each of you should look not only to your own interests, but also to the interests of others.

—Philippians 2:3–4

The point of uncovering financial infidelity in your Money Relationship isn't to point fingers or place blame. It's to help you and your spouse understand what's really happening in your relationship so that you can get rid of everything that's holding you back from a strong, healthy marriage.

In the same way that understanding your Money Personalities helps you and your spouse stop assuming the worst about each other, understanding how and why financial infidelity creeps into a relationship will allow you to name it and deal with it. That's how you get the trust back. That's how you grow closer as a couple. That's how you reclaim all those dreams you had.

Imagine a glass jar. Every time you commit financial infidelity, no matter how intentional or how innocent, no matter how much or how little money is involved, it's like adding a handful of rocks to that jar. Every handful crowds out the good stuff that makes a marriage work. The good news is that you can overcome financial infidelity. You can stop it, right now, then move forward by forgiving each other and building new patterns in your Money Relationship.

1. _____% of divorces are due to financial conflict.[2]

2. There are five root causes for financial infidelity:

   Cause #1 _____ _____

   Cause #2 _____ and _____

   Cause #3 _____ of _____

   Cause #4 _____

   Cause #5 _____ _____

Notes:

_____

_____

_____

_____

_____

INTERACTIVE DISCUSSION POINTS

1. Of the five causes of financial infidelity what do you think is the most common in our society?

_____

_____

2. "Expert Advice: Love by the Numbers; Your new marriage is bliss—until the bickering over finances begins. How to keep money from wrecking your home life"; [U.S. Edition Edition] Raina Kelley. *Newsweek*. New York: Apr 9, 2007. Vol. 149, Iss. 14; p. 48.

2. Did you notice any financial infidelity in the relationships you observed growing up?

_____

3. What Bible verse would help you when you are tempted to commit financial infidelity?

_____

_____

_____

_____

_____

_____

WEEKLY ACTIVITY

Every relationship has financial infidelity, but you can put an end to it once you become aware of where it exists in your relationship. Go to TheMoneyCouple.com and take the Financial Relationship Index quiz. It will help you determine how much financial infidelity exists in your marriage. Once you are aware of the kinds of financial infidelity in your marriage, use this week to pay attention to the ways they are creeping into your Money Relationship.

Day 1: _____

Day 2: _____

Day 3: _____

Day 4: _____

Day 5: Come together:

    a. Give one example of a time you have committed financial infidelity.

_____

_____

_____

    b. How will identifying financial infidelity improve your Money Relationship?

_____

_____

_____

    c. Make one commitment that can help end financial infidelity in your relationship. For example, agree to communicate about any purchase over $50, or agree to look over credit card statements together.

_____

_____

_____

Session 8

The Money Dump

Cast your cares on the LORD and he will sustain you; he will never let the righteous fall.
—Psalm 55:22

That's what the Money Dump is all about. It's a chance for you to dump out all the fears and worries and hopes you have for your Money Relationship. It's *not* the time to rip into your spouse or make a list of all his or her wrongdoings. You're not dumping *on* your spouse. You're dumping all the emotional crud inside you that is holding you back from really working *with* your spouse.

The Money Dump is also a way to celebrate the victories in your Money Relationship, no matter how insignificant they might seem. It's a way to name what's working so you can capitalize on your strengths. It's a way to show your spouse that you notice the contributions he or she makes to the family. It's a way to talk about what's really happening in your Money Relationship.

The Money Dump is a turning point for a lot of couples. For many of them, it's the first time they've gotten all these feelings about their Money Relationship out. It's the first time they've taken an honest look at what's working. And that feels really good. There's something cathartic about getting all that crud out of your system.

1. _____ _____ can be a catalyst to good conversation.

2. The Money Dump is all about "dumping out" pros and cons in our relationship as it relates to our:

   a. Money _____

   b. _____ Dynamic

   c. Financial _____

3. Celebrate the _____!

4. The seven steps to the Money Dump are:

   Step 1—Start in separate _____.

   Step 2—Write out the _____ and _____ of your money relationship.

   Step 3—Circle one _____.

   Step 4—Come together.

   Step 5—Read the _____ out loud.

   Step 6—Each share your _____ con.

   Step 7—For the next _____ days work on each con.

5. You just moved your relationship forward _____%.

6. While you can do a Money Dump as often as you like, be sure to have one at least once a _____.

Notes:

_____

_____

_____

_____

_____

INTERACTIVE DISCUSSION POINTS

1. What aspects of the Money Dump excite you?

_____

_____

_____

_____

2. What aspects of the Money Dump make you nervous?

_____

_____

_____

_____

3. Before you write down your Money Dump, take time to pray together. Pray for the following:

Open and honest communication

Patience with one another

Direction for your relationship

WEEKLY ACTIVITY

The Money Dump is an opportunity to "dump" the pros and the cons of your Money Relationship, including your Money Personalities, your Opposite Dynamic, and financial infidelity. Each day, take time to do the following:

Day 1: Write down three pros and cons of your Money
Personalities and your partner's Money Personalities.

	Name
Pros (example: you are great at saving money)	
Cons (example: you're inflexible with the budget)	

	Name
Pros (example: he or she is great at saving money)	
Cons (example: he or she is inflexible with the budget)	

Day 2: Write down three pros and cons of the Opposite Dynamic in your Money Relationship.

Pros (example: I don't feel like you support my home business)

_____

_____

_____

Cons (example: you help me take risks)

_____

_____

_____

Day 3: Write down three ways financial infidelity has affected your relationship.

_____

_____

_____

Day 4: Prayerfully consider one con that you want to work on for the next 90 days and circle it.

Day 5: Come together:

1. Read your pros out loud.

2. Each share your one con.

3. Acknowledge each other's con by saying to each other:

"I hear and understand that your con is _____ and I commit to supporting you as we build a stronger relationship."

Session 9
The Money Huddle

The body is a unit, though it is made up of many parts; and though all its parts are many, they form one body. So it is with Christ.
—1 Corinthians 12:12

The vast majority of the couples we meet are consumed by worry. They are worried about their debt. They are worried about their savings. They're worried about the future. And that worry is a big reason why their Money Relationships are a mess. They are so stressed out that even those little decisions about where to eat dinner or what kind of coffee to buy turn into major fights.

They think all that worry and stress is about their budget. But it's not. It's about their Money Relationship. No matter how much debt you have or how little money you have saved up, you can have a strong, healthy Money Relationship. But you have to be intentional about separating your financial situation from your Money Relationship. You're going to do that by using the Money Huddle.

The Money Huddle is not the time to balance your checkbook or pay your bills. It's not the time to gripe at your spouse about how much he spent getting the car detailed or blame your spouse for not keeping all of her receipts. It's not the time to look over your retirement plans or talk through potential investments. In other words, the Money Huddle is not the time to deal with your financial situation. Instead, the Money Huddle is a time to reconnect, to build trust, to work together to assess the present and dream about the future.

You've done a lot of hard work to get this far. Now it's time to take advantage of how far you've come and keep moving forward. When you set aside time each month to talk through the realities of your financial situation, to tell your spouse what you need in your Money Relationship, and to dream about the future together, you can put an end to fights, stop blaming each other, and grow closer than you've been in a long time.

1. According to a recent AP poll, _____% of Americans worry about debt all day, every day.[3]

2. Have a Money Huddle _____ minutes _____ a month.

3. A Money Huddle is not:

   - _____

   - _____

   - _____

4. A Money Huddle is:

   - _____

   - _____

   - _____

3. Stephen Covey says, "Begin with the _____ in mind."

---

3. http://collectionagencymedia.com/press/indebted-americans-spend-3-5-hours-a-day
-worrying-about-debt/.

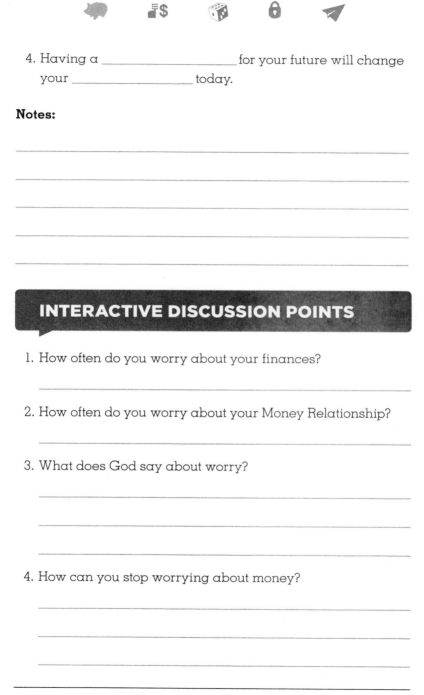

4. Having a _____ for your future will change
   your _____ today.

Notes:

_____

_____

_____

_____

_____

INTERACTIVE DISCUSSION POINTS

1. How often do you worry about your finances?

_____

2. How often do you worry about your Money Relationship?

_____

3. What does God say about worry?

_____

_____

_____

4. How can you stop worrying about money?

_____

_____

_____

WEEKLY ACTIVITY

For the next four days, write down one of your money worries.

Day 1: _____

Day 2: _____

Day 3: _____

Day 4: _____

Day 5: Come together: Read your worries to each other. This is not a time to blame but a time to understand the other person's concerns.

_____

_____

_____

_____

_____

_____

_____

Session 10

Begin with the E.N.D. in Mind

For God has not given us a spirit of fear, but of power and of love and of a sound mind.
—2 Timothy 1:7 (NKJV)

In his bestselling book *The 7 Habits of Highly Effective People*, late author Stephen Covey suggests that those who want to be successful in life should "begin with the end in mind."[4] That's certainly true when it comes to your Money Relationship.

You need to have a vision for what your Money Relationship could look like. We find that most couples have a fairly simple vision. They want to stop fighting. They want a Money Relationship in which they work together instead of battling each other. They want to make decisions without arguing and solve problems without blame. They want harmony instead of conflict. So what do you want?

Once you have a vision for your Money Relationship, you have to be intentional about making that vision a reality. You have to be committed to developing new patterns of communication. You have to be willing to give up some longstanding habits. And you have to be willing to talk about your Money Relationship.

---

4. Covey, Stephen R. *The Seven Habits of Highly Effective People: Restoring the Character Ethic* (New York: Free Press, 2004).

1. Get along, every day, when it comes to _____ .

2. Use the acronym _____ to direct your Money Huddles.

3. Each component of your Money Huddle only takes _____ minutes:

   E. _____ your Savings and your Debt.

   N. _____ have to be expressed.

   D. _____ together!

Notes:

_____

_____

_____

_____

INTERACTIVE DISCUSSION POINTS

1. Why are Money Huddles important in our relationship?

   _____

   _____

2. On what day of the month are we going to commit to having our Money Huddles? Suggestion: Make it easy to remember and plan for—the first Sunday, the last Saturday, etc.

   _____

3. How will our Money Huddles impact our family?

_____

_____

_____

4. Second Timothy 1:7 says, "For God has not given us a spirit of fear, but of power and of love and of a sound mind." How can we exemplify this in our Money Huddles?

_____

_____

_____

WEEKLY ACTIVITY

We would like you to go into your first Money Huddle prepared. This week's activities are designed to do just that:

Day 1: Separately write down the amount of debt and savings you have in the relationship.

Debt: _____

Savings: _____

Day 2: Separately write down the money needs you have for yourself and your family.

Needs (take your con list into consideration):

_____

_____

_____

Day 3: Write down your dreams about the following:

Vacations: _____

_____

Retirement (when the paycheck stops): _____

_____

Charity: _____

Other: _____

Day 4: Congratulate yourself.

Day 5: Bring your lists from your first four days and have your first Money Huddle together.

Notes from the Evaluation (savings and debt):

_____

_____

_____

Notes from expressing Needs (take your con list into consideration):

_____

_____

_____

Notes about Dreams:

_____

_____

_____

Session 11

Why We Fight

They sharpen their tongues like swords and aim their words like deadly arrows.
—Psalm 64:3

Love is patient, love is kind. It does not envy, it does not boast, it is not proud. It does not dishonor others, it is not self-seeking, it is not easily angered, it keeps no record of wrongs. Love does not delight in evil but rejoices with the truth. It always protects, always trusts, always hopes, always perseveres.
—1 Corinthians: 13:4–7 (UPDATED NIV)

Arguments about money hurt us like very few other fights. They feel intensely personal. We feel attacked and get defensive. We walk away from them filled with anger, resentment, and a deep sense of mistrust. For a long time, we didn't understand why money fights seemed to create such complex, long-term problems for couples. But when we thought about how deeply embedded our Money Personalities are, it all started to make sense. If you and your spouse want to prevent money arguments from reaching that hurtful level, you have to respect each other's Money Personalities and avoid making them the center of your conflicts.

And even with all the new information and tools you've got, you are still two people with two different perspectives on money. You are going to make decisions your spouse doesn't understand. And your spouse is going to make decisions you don't understand. But when you feel close to your spouse, when you know you've got shared goals and dreams for your future, then you don't want to hurt each other. And when you do hurt each other, you want to make it right. That's what happens when your Money Relationship is working.

1. It is no secret that money _____ are running _____ in our relationships.

2. We _____ our spouses for their Money Personalities.

3. Root Reason #1—We don't know and _____ our Money Personalities.

4. Root Reason #2—We commit _____ _____.

Notes:

_____

_____

_____

_____

_____

INTERACTIVE DISCUSSION POINTS

1. How often do you and your spouse argue about money? (example: once a week, once a month, once a year)

_____

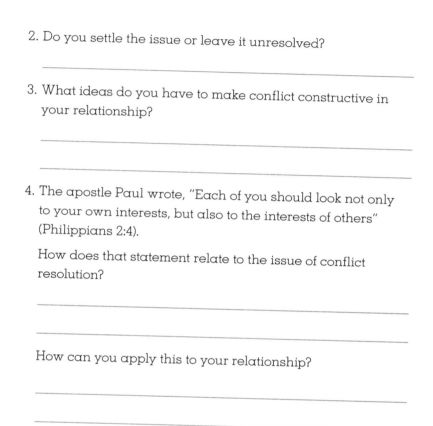

2. Do you settle the issue or leave it unresolved?

_____

3. What ideas do you have to make conflict constructive in your relationship?

_____

_____

4. The apostle Paul wrote, "Each of you should look not only to your own interests, but also to the interests of others" (Philippians 2:4).

How does that statement relate to the issue of conflict resolution?

_____

_____

How can you apply this to your relationship?

_____

_____

WEEKLY ACTIVITY

Our goal is for you to bring your love and money together. Bringing up past hurts and disagreements does not move you forward as a couple. This week we want you to reflect on what you love and appreciate about each other.

Day 1: I appreciate the following about my spouse:

_____

_____

Day 2: I appreciate the following about my spouse:

_____

_____

Day 3: I appreciate the following about my spouse:

_____

_____

Day 4: I appreciate the following about my spouse:

_____

_____

Day 5: Come together: Read your "appreciation lists" to each other.

Session 12

Stop, Drop, and Roll

Do not be anxious about anything, but in every situation, by prayer and petition, with thanksgiving, present your requests to God. And the peace of God, which transcends all understanding, will guard your hearts and your minds in Christ Jesus.

—**Philippians 4:6–7** (UPDATED NIV)

Understand this, my dear brothers and sisters: You must all be quick to listen, slow to speak, and slow to get angry.

—**James 1:19** (NLT)

No matter what your Money Personalities, no matter what your past looks like, no matter how committed you are to building a better future, you are going to have disagreements about money. But what you do with those disagreements is what separates the average marriage from a great marriage.

So many of the couples we work with have forgotten how to compromise. But once you have learned about each other's Money Personalities, once you've started expressing your needs in your Money Huddles, once you've begun the repair work on your Money Relationship, finding a way forward that will satisfy both of you becomes a whole lot easier.

1. The *New York Times* recently reported that couples who fought about money more than once a week were _____% more likely to get divorced.[5]

2. Money _____ are the most destructive fights you can have.

3. Steps to Fighting Fair:

   #1 Stop, Drop and _____

   #2 See what is _____

   #3 _____

Notes:

_____

_____

_____

_____

_____

_____

_____

_____

_____

_____

_____

_____

_____

_____

5. http://economix.blogs.nytimes.com/2009/12/07/money-fights-predict-divorce-rates/.

Read the following scenario and evaluate how the couple could Stop, Drop, and Roll:

After their Money Huddle, Suzie and Kyle agreed they needed to save more. Kyle came home with new camping equipment. Suzie was furious. She said, "We agreed we weren't going to buy any more extras." Kyle said, "But we *need* new camping equipment." Suzie continued to exacerbate the situation by saying, "You always spend, you don't care about us, you don't care about our family."

Read the following scenario and evaluate how the couple could see what is real:

Last week Tom came home to find a huge package on the front door of the house. It was from a large retail store, even though he and Suzanne had agreed in their last Money Huddle that they were no longer going to do online shopping. Suzanne was not home from work yet. What should Tom do?

Read the following scenario and evaluate how the couple could compromise:

Steve has come home from a job interview that went great. He is looking to change careers and seize this as an opportunity of a lifetime. Katie is worried because Steve will no longer have a fixed income but will transition to commission. How should they compromise?

WEEKLY ACTIVITY

We want this last week to be a time to bring all components of this *5 Money Personalities* DVD-based study together.

Day 1: How has understanding your Money Personalities changed your relationship?

_____

_____

_____

Day 2: How has understanding the Opposite Dynamic changed your relationship?

_____

_____

_____

Day 3: What is the day you have settled on for your Money Huddles?

_____

_____

_____

Day 4: Come together: Share your reflections from the last three days.

_____

_____

_____

_____

Day 5: Watch Session 13 and . . . "Make It Happen"!

RICHARD SCARRY'S

Find Your ABC's

STERLING and the distinctive Sterling logo are
registered trademarks of Sterling Publishing Co., Inc.

Library of Congress Cataloging-in-Publication Data

Scarry, Richard.
Richard Scarry's find your ABC's / Richard Scarry.
p. cm.
"This book was originally published in 1973 by Random House, Inc."–Copyright p.
Summary: With the help of the reader, two detectives search for the letters of the alphabet.
ISBN 978-1-4027-6294-9
[1. Mystery and detective stories. 2. Animals–Fiction. 3. Alphabet.] I. Title. II. Title: Find your ABC's.
PZ7.S327Fi 2009
[E]--dc22
2008018636

2 4 6 8 10 9 7 5 3

Published in 2008 by Sterling Publishing Co., Inc.
387 Park Avenue South, New York, NY 10016
In association with JB Communications, Inc.
6 West 37th Street, 4th Floor, New York, NY 10018
On behalf of the Richard Scarry Corporation
This book was originally published in 1973 by Random House, Inc.
© 1973 Richard Scarry
Copyright renewed 2001 by Richard Scarry 2nd.
Copyright assigned to Richard Scarry Corporation
Distributed in Canada by Sterling Publishing
c/o Canadian Manda Group, 165 Dufferin Street
Toronto, Ontario, Canada M6K 3H6
Distributed in the United Kingdom by GMC Distribution Services
Castle Place, 166 High Street, Lewes, East Sussex, England BN7 1XU
Distributed in Australia by Capricorn Link (Australia) Pty. Ltd.
P.O. Box 704, Windsor, NSW 2756, Australia

Printed in China
All rights reserved

Designed by Elizabeth Azen

Sterling ISBN 978-1-4027-6294-9

For information about custom editions, special sales, premium
and corporate purchases, please contact Sterling Special Sales Department
at 800-805-5489 or specialsales@sterlingpublishing.com.

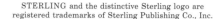

RICHARD SCARRY'S

Find
Your
ABC's

STERLING

New York / London

This is Sam. This is Dudley.

They are two very fine detectives. Sam and Dudley can find almost anything. Sometimes they fix themselves up so nobody will recognize them. They wear disguises.

Look at that sack of potatoes. Would you think it was a detective looking for something? No! Of course not. But it is. That sack of potatoes is Sam, in disguise!

And who is this lady putting on lipstick? Would you believe that it isn't a lady at all? It's Dudley, in *his* disguise!

But what are Sam and Dudley looking for now? They are looking for all the letters in the alphabet. Will YOU help them?

As you read this book you will find that words for many objects and characters are printed near them.

On each page a new letter of the alphabet is featured in these words in color.

Why not put on your disguise and help Sam and Dudley hunt for all these letters?

On the last page, you will find out what Sam and Dudley do with them.

A a

artist

painting

oak

can

apples

p n

antenna

ax

pail

Sam and Dudley have disguised themselves.

hat

glasses

grass

an angry ant

arrow

tractor

road

splash

weather vane

barn

balloon

tail

Alfred Alligator

aviator

airplane

falling leaf

Can you help them find all of the big "A's" and small "a's"?

laundry

feather

cabbage patch

rake

wagon

After you have found them, put them in Sam's sack, then turn the page and look for the next letters.

B b

bird

bell

broom

Captain Bob

blue boat

BARBER BAKERY

buildings

Albert Bug

ball

bunny baby

BEWARE

boy

buoy

Sam and Dudley have driven to the harbor.
Dudley forgot to step on the brake!
Look where they have landed! They will
have trouble finding big "B's" and little
"b's" while they are in the water.
Can YOU find them?

box

Cc

cone

raccoon

cap

church

clock

Captain Crocodile

cane

canoe

Look at that crazy accident! A cat's coat is going to be covered with ketchup. Put your "C's" into Sam's wet sack, and let's go on.

cherries

cucumber

corn

ketchup

carrot

grocer

crate

crane

GROCERIES

Dd

a delicious hot dog with mustard

HOT DOGS

Drink Lemonade!

door

Sam and Dudley have driven down to the sandy beach. Can you help them find all of the "D's"?

Daddy

sand

doll

daisy

head

diaper

derrick

dump truck

Doctor Dog bandaging a head

hot dog

bandage

Tillie, the deep-water diver

E e

elm tree

Edward Leopard,
a very excited
life saver

shower

umbrella

TOILETS
← ENTER
HERE

dressing rooms

reel

EXTRA

Father sleeping

eyeglasses

needles

thread

shovel

seashell

And where is Detective Dudley?
Is he in a dressing room? I don't think so.
He must be looking for "E's."
Try to find Dudley and all the "E's."

eleven sand fleas fleeing

waves

elephant

speedboat

E8

submarine

Ff

forest

Freddy Fox

flag

fence

Farmer Alfalfa

A fire has broken out at Farmer Alfalfa's farm. Five firemen have come to put it out. In the river a funny frog is looking for "F's."

a flaming football

fire engine

fruit

five firemen

Fresh Fruit a

fisherman

funny frog

ferryboat

four fish

G g

Goodness gracious! Grandma's wagon got knocked over. Dudley is looking for "G's." Have *you* found any? When you have found Dudley and all the "G's," Sam has a good riddle for you.

grapes

grapes

Grandma Pig

wagon

glasses

awning

Gertie Goose

engine

a young girl goat

eggs

big jug

bag

vegetables

green grass

bridge

Here is Sam's good riddle: What has two feet and flies? Do you know the answer? Do you give up? Well, the answer is– Dudley, disguised as a garbage can!

garbage can

H h

Tillie and Miss Honey, the schoolteacher, are having a lawn party for the children. Hear the orchestra happily playing. But Sam is high in the air, about to hit the shortcake. Can he be gathering "H's"?

Tillie

Heavens!

Miss Honey

Horrors!

heel

hat

head

hat

Harry Heron

horn

harmonica

Henny Hen

harp

Homer Hedgehog

feather

chair

I i

tiny insect

Did you invite HIM?

ice cream

Ichabod Fish

tire

dish

knife

pie

a frightened alligator

Impossible Driver!

Where is Dudley going in such a hurry? He is an impossible driver, isn't he? He should stop his automobile while looking for "I's."

J j

a jolly
jack-o-lantern

Janitor Joe

Just look at the jumble!
Janitor Joe enjoys jolting
journeys in his pajamas.

jeep

Look! Sam has put on a new disguise.
Now he is a big cake on a bike. Yum-yum!

K k

cake

kerchief

fork

cook in
back of truck

bike

Kate Kitty

KATE'S
BAKERY

Kid Kelly
skating to kindergarten

Hi, Kid!

truck

stick

NO
PARKING

L l

flashing light

Louie, the policeman

tall lamp

taillight

POLICE

ladder

manhole

Well, see where Dudley landed! He didn't look where he was going. He is disguised as three-flavored ice cream from Tillie's lawn party. Be careful, Dudley! Children like to eat delicious ice cream!

GO LEFT

yellow line

mail box

a yelling mailman

letters

a little girl

sidewalk

Now...has everyone found all the "L's" to put in Sam's sack?

M m

helmet

hammer

Foolish Fox, the mechanic

mop

broom

motorcycle

Mother Goose

Mr. Foolish Fox, the mechanic, is hammering the bumps out of Dudley's car.
Sam has made himself a new disguise to wear while he looks for "M's."

smokestack

locomotive

milk carton

MILK

Mrs. Mouse

platform

N n

Dudley can't fool anyone in his new disguise.
A lot of people already think he's a nut!
But a nice, lovable, funny sort of nut, of course.

Look out, Dudley!

That hungry elephant likes peanuts.

sun

handle

frying pan

signal

nut

hungry elephant's trunk

passenger train

bent nail

conductor

Ned Lion

urse Bella

CANDY

NO SNORING IN THE STATION

SANDWICHES

newsboy

hand car

trunk

Oscar Crow

OK

Oswald Owl

old cannon

soldier

fort

Ole Octopus is rowing his old, hole-y rowboat
out to the queen's palace. His two funny-looking
passengers seem to be on the lookout for "O's."

Ole Octopus

a round orange

a coil of rope

bottom of
the ocean

rowboat

The round orange on the rowboat shouts,
"I can see four 'O's' in the 'bottom of the ocean,' Dudley."

Pp

pennant

spaghetti

palace

Papa Peter

PAPA PETER'S PIZZA PARLOR

portal

steps

painter

purple paint

The people at the palace are very pleased to see the passengers on the rowboat. Papa Peter has made a platter of slippery spaghetti for them.

Qq

Squire Quigley

quiver

The Squirming Quartet

As they quit the quay, the queen quickly asks a question: "Have you all been minding your 'P's' and your 'Q's'? Have you?"

quay

1 Quart

The queen is quaffing a quart of quince juice.

R r

What is the best disguise to wear at an airport?
An airplane disguise, of course!

control tower

radio

READER AIRPORT

REST ROOMS

Captain Roger

engineer

first officer

waiting room

four furious crew members

stewardess

helicoptor

parachu

There are so many airplanes here
that nobody will ever discover
Dudley searching for "R's."

crash landing

rear door

SWIFTAIR

front door

stairs

ground crewman

aviator

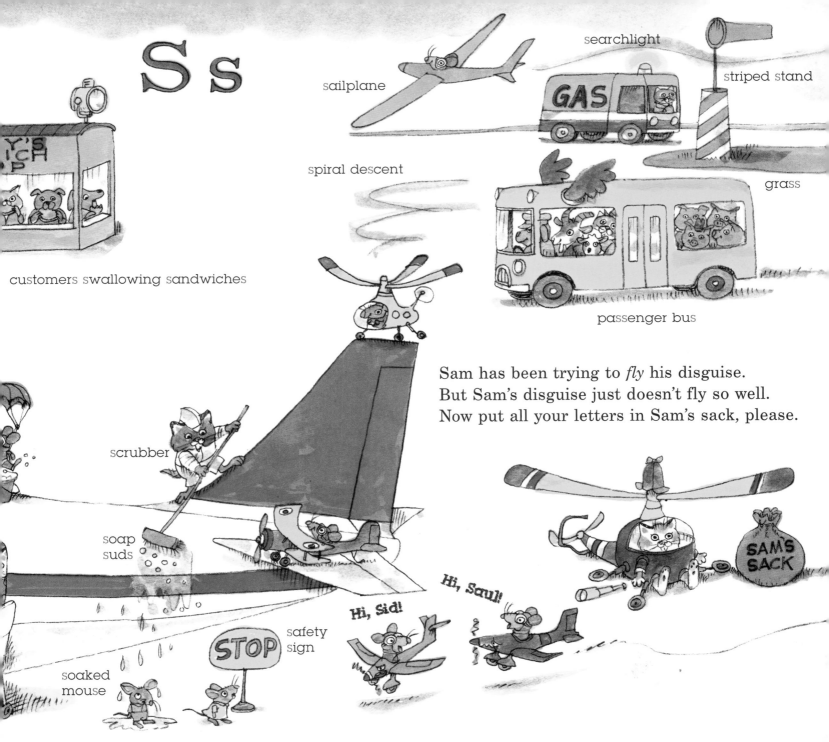

S s

searchlight

striped stand

sailplane

GAS

spiral descent

grass

customers swallowing sandwiches

passenger bus

Sam has been trying to *fly* his disguise.
But Sam's disguise just doesn't fly so well.
Now put all your letters in Sam's sack, please.

scrubber

soap suds

SAM'S SACK

Hi, Saul!

Hi, Sid!

STOP safety sign

soaked mouse

T t

tree

tomato

TOM TAILOR

TED BUTCHER

TINA'S TOYS

meat

Sergeant Murphy

STOP!

hydrant

traffic light

dent

Two turtles are traveling through the tiny town. Look! Their little car has hit a little tomato cart. SPLAT! Twenty-two thousand tomatoes have been spilt!

cart

telephone booth

TELEPHONE

Neat Timothy, the street cleaner, has fainted.

Tom Tiger

U u

umbrella

Uncle Louie

underwear

HOUSE OF MUSIC

UNIFORMS

SUBWAY

nurse

Uncle Louie jumped up in the air.
But his suit stayed behind.

Can you find any
"T's" and "U's" under
all those tomatoes?

Uriah Duck
ducking

dump truck

blue suit

mud

curb

V v

V-a-r-o-o-m! Have you ever seen such driving? NO! Never, ever!

violin

vase

shovel

VINNY and VIKKI MOVERS
"WE LOVE TO MOVE"

Vinny, the driver

lovely Virginia's violent vacuum cleaner

vine

violets

five leaves

clover

CURVE

Victor Dove

river

gravy boat

Ww

woods

Wilber Crow

Willy Wolf, the witty woodchopper, is working along the wayside. Suddenly he whistles wildly. "Well," he says, "I have seen cars drive in the woods, but I have never seen woods drive in a car."

strawberries

yellow vest

Walter Walrus wearing a watch at his wrist

Haw! Haw! Haw!

GO SLOW

wheel

wood

two wrestlers

Xx

Max Ox doesn't exactly watch where he is going. He needs to have his eyes examined.

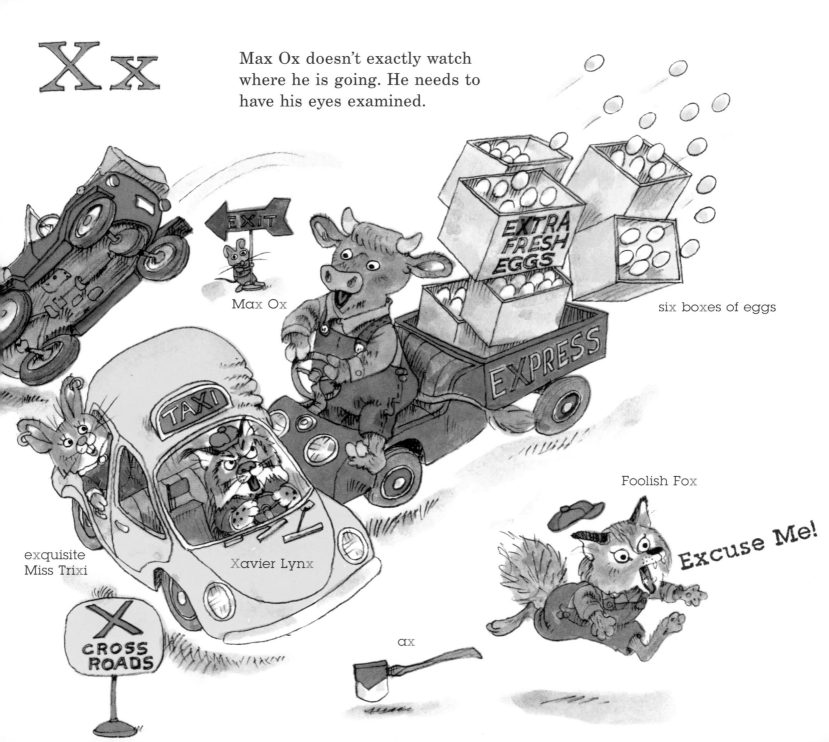

Max Ox

six boxes of eggs

EXTRA FRESH EGGS

EXPRESS

EXIT

Foolish Fox

exquisite Miss Trixi

Xavier Lynx

TAXI

X CROSS ROADS

ax

Excuse Me!

Yy

hydrant

ONE WAY

Harry Hyena

Yum! Yum!

yellow
yolk

frying pan

Yikes!

Yvonne Kitty

Harry Hyena is very hungry.
Why is he suddenly so happy?

Zip, the postman

SAM'S SACK

Sam's pants,
unzipped

zipper

zebra

Bugdozer

Z z

Izzy and Zelda Lizard

At last we have come to the last letter of the alphabet—"Z."
Find the "Z's" and finish putting your letters in Sam's sack.
Just a minute! Sam's pants are unzipped. Zip up your pants,
Sam, so you can walk.

Aa Bb Cc Dd

Ii Jj Kk Ll

Qq Rr Ss Tt

Uu Vv Ww Xx

Yy Zz

" 'ey, 'arry! You're dropping your 'H's'!"
"I know, 'enry. I can't 'elp it.
It's a bad 'abit I 'ave!"

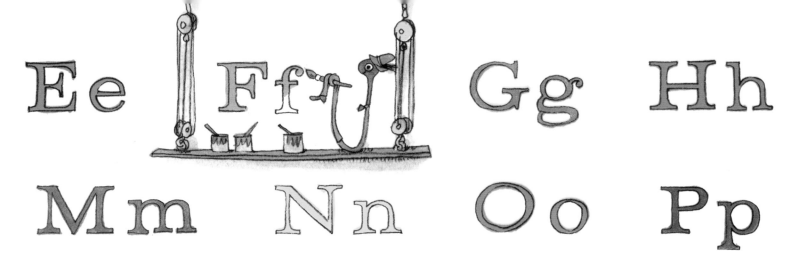

Ee Ff Gg Hh
Mm Nn Oo Pp

Ah! There is Lowly Worm painting all the letters of the alphabet.
And what are Sam and Dudley doing with all the letters we
have found? They are making an *alphabet soup!* That's what
they are doing. Stanley is slowly stirring the soup.

Mmmmmm! It does smell good.

Now...let's all sit down and eat it.
Say!!! Who put the shoe in the alphabet soup?
That's not a shoe! That's Lowly Worm in disguise.
All right, Mister Shoe-please get out of the soup.
You're not a letter of the alphabet!

A Beginner's Guide to Technical Communication

McGraw-Hill's *BEST*—Basic Engineering Series and Tools

A Beginner's Guide to Technical Communication

Anne Eisenberg
Polytechnic University

WCB McGraw-Hill

Boston, Massachusetts   Burr Ridge, Illinois   Dubuque, Iowa
Madison, Wisconsin   New York, New York   San Francisco, California   St. Louis, Missouri

WCB/McGraw-Hill
*A Division of the **McGraw-Hill** Companies*

A BEGINNER'S GUIDE TO TECHNICAL COMMUNICATION

This book is printed on acid-free paper.

7 8 9 0 DOC/DOC 0 9 8 7

ISBN: 978-0-07-092045-3
MHID: 0-07-092045-1

Vice president and editorial director: *Kevin Kane*
Publisher: *Tom Casson*
Executive editor: *Eric Munson*
Developmental editor II: *Holly Stark*
Marketing manager: *John T. Wannemacher*
Project manager: *Kari A. Geltemeyer*
Production supervisor: *Heather D. Burbridge*
Senior designer: *Laurie J. Entringer*
Cover designer: *Heidi J. Baughman*
Cover image: *Nola López / Graphistock*
Compositor: *York Graphic Services, Inc.*
Typeface: *10/12 Century Schoolbook*
Printer: *R. R. Donnelley & Sons Company*

Library of Congress Cataloging-in-Publication Data

Eisenberg, Anne
    Beginner's guide to technical communication / Anne Eisenberg.—
1st ed.
        p. cm.—(McGraw-Hill's BEST—basic engineering series and
tools)
    Includes index.
    ISBN 0-07-092045-1
    1. Communication of technical information. I. Title.
II. Series.
T10.5.E358 1998
    808'.066—dc21   97-24522

http://www.mhhe.com/engineering/general/best

About the Author

Anne Eisenberg writes regularly for *Scientific American.* A professor at Polytechnic University in Brooklyn, New York, she is the author of four other textbooks, including *Effective Technical Communication* published by McGraw-Hill. She has wide experience teaching technical writing and editing for the American Chemical Society as well as for many U.S. companies.

Welcome to McGraw-Hill's *BEST*—Basic Engineering Series and Tools

Foreword

Engineering educators have had long-standing debates over the content of introductory freshman engineering courses. Some schools emphasize computer-based instruction, some focus on engineering analysis, some concentrate on graphics and visualization, while others emphasize hands-on design. Two things, however, appear certain: no two schools do exactly the same thing, and at most schools, the introductory engineering courses frequently change from one year to the next. In fact, the introductory engineering courses at many schools have become a smorgasbord of different topics, some classical and others closely tied to computer software applications. Given this diversity in content and purpose, the task of providing appropriate text material becomes problematic, since every instructor requires something different.

McGraw-Hill has responded to this challenge by creating a series of modularized textbooks for the topics covered in most first-year introductory engineering courses. Written by authors who are acknowledged authorities in their respective fields, the individual modules vary in length, in accordance with the time typically devoted to each subject. For example, modules on programming languages are written as introductory-level textbooks, providing material for an entire semester of study, whereas modules that cover shorter topics such as ethics and technical writing provide less material, as appropriate for a few weeks of instruction. Individual instructors can easily combine these modules to conform to their particular courses. Most modules include numerous problems and/or projects, and are suitable for use within an active-learning environment.

Welcome to McGraw-Hill's *BEST*—Basic Engineering Series and Tools

The goal of this series is to provide the educational community with text material that is timely, affordable, of high quality, and flexible in how it is used. We ask that you assist us in fulfilling this goal by letting us know how well we are serving your needs. We are particularly interested in knowing what, in your opinion, we have done well, and where we can make improvements to offer new modules.

Byron S. Gottfried
Consulting Editor
University of Pittsburgh

Preface

This book is a beginner's guide to writing reports and other technical communication.

It will help you learn how to think through, organize, write, and revise assignments for your freshman engineering class, or for any first-, second-, or third-year class that requires scientific or technical reports.

The book is written so that you can use it on your own if you are not yet taking a technical communications course. There are many examples.

It is the first book of its kind—all the examples are patterned on writing done in first-year engineering classes.

This book has three parts: chapters to read before you write; chapters to read while you write; and chapters to read after you write.

Before You Write

Chapter 1 discusses the logical structure of reports, and the kind of information that belongs in each part. You'll see models of each part of the report, including the abstract, the introduction, the procedure, the results, and the discussion. The examples have an original version, with typical errors, and a revised version that the writer has improved. Comments on the improvements are written in the margin.

Chapter 2 has examples of longer reports. The first example is a report on the functions of the oscilloscope. The original version of this report is not coherent. In the revised version, the sections of the report flow logically from one another. The second example is a report on an apparatus (an optical microscope) and an experiment using the apparatus to characterize a substance. Next to the report are comments explaining how the report is organized, and why the organization is effective.

While You Write

Chapter 3 discusses strategies to help you transform the raw materials of an experiment into a report. These techniques will help you get past the particularly tough parts in writing: assimilating the data, getting started, and avoiding roadblocks along the way.

- From brainstorming with teammates to keeping a laboratory notebook, there are many tactics you can use to turn report format to your advantage as you begin drafting your report.
- All the strategies are ones students in first-year engineering programs say are helpful in keeping up the impetus as they start to write, maintaining the accuracy and logic of the content, and focusing their attention as they go through initial drafts of the report.

After You Write

Chapters 4 and 5 discuss ways to edit your document. Once you've articulated your main points and organized them, you will want to look word-by-word at your document, trimming and focusing the language so that your message is as clear as possible. Chapters 4 and 5 discuss trouble spots in style, usage, grammar, and punctuation (For instance, use of first person, ways to expand definitions, governing tense, and representation of numbers). Some issues are the same as in your English class, but others (such as tense, representation of numbers, and rapid changes in compound words and hyphenation) are quite different.

The author thanks the students and staff of the Freshman Engineering program at Polytechnic University for their help—in particular, Charles A. Kelly (director of freshman engineering), Steven Gellar, Carlos Mejia, and Michael Connell (teaching assistants in freshman engineering), Professor Donald Scarl, inventor of the thermal insulation competition that appears in Chapter 1, Professor Nancy Tooney, Professor Bruce Garetz, and William F. Auffermann, whose fine report is in Chapter 2.

Anne Eisenberg

Contents

A Beginner's Guide to Technical Communication

The Logical Structure of Technical Reports—Section by Section

Outline

What Is a Report?

A report is an objective account of events that you witnessed—of events that you saw firsthand and then recounted to others.

The word *report* comes from ancient words meaning *to bear* or *bring back*—in a technical report, you are bearing or bringing back news of something that you observed.

The format or shape of reports is an ancient one; the format originated in antiquity, probably for forensic investigations. Then and now, reports had to meet a basic test: *they had to be verifiable.*

What does it mean to be verifiable? It means that if you do your report properly, your description will be so *objective* that any skilled person following the steps you describe will get similar results—that is, the person will be able to *replicate* your work.

What Are the Parts of a Report?

In a report of an experiment, the parts are traditionally divided into five parts: an abstract, an introduction, a procedural section, a results section, and a discussion/conclusions section.

1. An abstract. This is a short statement of what you intended to do (your *objective*), what you found out (your *results*), and what the results mean (your *conclusions and implications*). An abstract is a synopsis of the findings and their significance.

In some laboratory classes, students are asked to substitute a *statement of objective and scope* in place of a full abstract. If this is the case in your class, instead of writing a full abstract, give the goal and range of the experiment, but omit findings and implications.

2. An introduction. An introduction steps back and tells the reader the *problem* or *issue* you addressed and the *significance* of the problem. Sometimes you will include short references to *related literature* (published studies or reports by other people who have investigated the same problem). Although the introduction may be quite short—often one or two paragraphs are adequate—it is a crucial section, for it gives the background to the work you will report.

3. A procedural section. A procedural section tells what you did (the steps you took in doing the experiment or investigation) in such detail that other skilled people could follow the same steps and replicate your work. It may include a description of the *apparatus* you used unless it is standard, the *materials* you used, and the *steps* that you took (the method).

In some laboratory classes, the apparatus, materials, and procedure are already printed in the manual; in this case, it is unnecessary to repeat the printed account of the process in the procedural section of your report. As the examples in the chapter will show, in cases like this, tell what you did *in relation to the printed procedure,* rather than simply transcribing what is already in print.

In general, if part of your procedure is standard—that is, if the details are published elsewhere—give the reference that will lead the reader to the publication, rather than repeating the details. If you adapted the procedure, describe any details that distinguish what you did from the standard method.

The procedural section may be called *Experimental Work, Experimental, Methods, Methods and Materials,* or simply *Procedure.*

The voice that you use in the procedure—active voice or passive voice—depends on the style you choose.

Using the passive voice ("The image was rotated.") puts the emphasis on the object (the image), rather than on the subject (you, the person who did the rotating).

Using the active voice ("We rotated the image.") places the emphasis on you, the doer.

Using active voice, though, presents a problem. When you turn to active voice, you'll often have to accompany it with the first-person pronouns *we* and *I* ("We examined the spectra."). Why is this a problem? Engineers and scientists tend to avoid the use of *I*, even though standard references like the *American Chemical Society Style Guide* say that first person is perfectly acceptable. (Chapter 4, "First-person pronouns," gives reasons.) Engineers and scientists will, however, accept the use of *we.* Many people in technology and business now routinely use *we*, preferring the emphasis it gives to their voices.

But while *we* has growing acceptability, *I* is still questioned by many. Therefore, if you have a choice between using *I* and a passive voice in the procedure, you are usually safer going with convention and using the passive voice.

4. A results section. The results summarize your findings, usually in two ways:

With visuals, in tables, graphs, and other figures that summarize the data graphically.

With a narrative, in a passage where you explain in words the key results that people will need to follow your conclusions.

This section is sometimes called *Data/Observations,* rather than *Results.* In some laboratory classes, the results sections are combined with the discussion section, and called *Results and Discussion, Results and Conclusions,* or *Findings and Discussion.*

In the results section, include a summary of the data and, when appropriate, a discussion of the computational or statistical methods used. Cite any references for the statistical methods on first mention. Also identify and describe any computational methods employed, including computerized analyses. Include sufficient results to justify your conclusions. Use tables and graphs to display data vividly and concisely. Check to ensure that the information in the tables and figures is consistent with information in the text.

5. A discussion/conclusions section. The discussion section steps back to answer the question, Did you solve the problem you initially set out to conquer? To do this, you'll need to

- Explain any experimental difficulties relevant to the conclusions.
- Discuss inconsistencies in measurement.
- Interpret and compare your results.
- Point out special features of the argument.
- Link this discussion explicitly to your objectives.

If you have sufficient evidence, follow with conclusions or inferences based on the evidence and then, when appropriate, with recommendations for future work.

What Style of Writing Is Best in Reports?

Reports should be written as directly, clearly, and simply as possible. Their tone should be objective rather than subjective.

To maintain an objective tone,

- Concentrate on presenting facts rather than feelings.
- Avoid jokes and asides that may turn the attention of the reader toward you rather than toward the argument you are discussing.
- Resist taking emotion-laden positions on the information that you are presenting.

In general, writers of technical reports try to minimize the injection of their personality into the text. Instead, they keep their attention on the logic of the argument and on the data that support the argument.

As to the overall style of reports, John Maynard Keynes said that Isaac Newton's works showed "careful learning, accurate method, and extreme sobriety of statement." This last characteristic, "extreme sobriety of statement," sums up the basic style of reports then and now.

Can You Be Persuasive in a Report?

Reports are traditionally objective in their style, but that doesn't mean that you can't persuade the reader of your argument.

In fact, the whole structure of the report attempts to convince readers that the author has done a methodical job of analyzing the data and has come up with reasonable conclusions.

Leo Szilard, the great physicist, once joked about the persuasiveness of his reports, "Certainly God knows the facts, but does he know *my version* of the facts?"

Reports are always the writer's version of the facts, and thus are inherently persuasive within the limits of scientific style.

What Questions Should You Answer in a Report of an Investigation or of an Experiment?

In a report of an investigation or experiment, you should address these questions:

1. What did you do? (your objective)
2. Why did you do it? (the introduction or background)
3. How did you do it? (the procedure)
4. What did you find out? (the results)

5. What do the findings mean? (the conclusions and recommendations)

It's very important to logically link the sections of the report to one another. For instance, if you are writing a report on basic controls and operations of an oscilloscope, and you examine three different operations, your report must explicitly connect the description in the introduction (the problem) to the description of what you did (the procedure), and then, in turn, to the description in the results and discussion (what you found out about the problem). One of Chapter 2's examples (a report on the oscilloscope) shows the difference between sections of a report that are linked together logically and sections of a report that are not.

Is the Investigative Pattern the Only Way to Organize Reports?

Most engineering reports fit into the investigative pattern—engineers are problem solvers, and their reports usually document how they worked their way toward a solution—but some reports do not. For instance, you may be reviewing the literature of a field or comparing different types of software.

For reports that are outside the experimental format,

- Include an abstract and an introduction.
- Divide the body of the report according to the subject matter. For instance, if you are reporting on a series of examples or cases, divide the body of the report into Case 1, Case 2, and Case 3. Once you have defined the three cases, divide the text again, for instance, into Advantages and Disadvantages. Then compare and contrast Advantages and Disadvantages. Follow with conclusions and, when requested, recommendations.

Regardless of whether the report presents research results or, for instance, reviews the literature of a field, the report must establish main points before introducing detail. To do this effectively, start with an abstract or summary that gives the objective, the findings, and the implications. Use the introduction to sum up the problem and its significance and, when appropriate, to show how the present work adds to or differs from related work on the problem.

Divide the body of the report logically using headings and subheadings to show the reader the path of the argument. Keep the body of the report as lean as possible, using tables for vivid, concise display of data and graphs for trends.

If you aren't sure how to divide the body of the report logically, imagine a three-part structure:

The front section

Introduces a problem or issue and its significance.
Gives scope and limits.

Summarizes related work in the field when appropriate.

Concludes with a roadmap or guide to the contents that follow.

The body

Presents major arguments and supporting evidence.

Analyzes evidence supporting the arguments.

Draws conclusions and implications.

The back section

Supports the body with references and attachments such as spread sheets or calculations.

A formal report (for instance, one written after a semester's work on a project) might include

Front section:

Title page

Table of contents

List of figures/illustrations

List of tables/charts

Abstract

Body:

Introduction (statement of purpose, conditions under which work was done, general background, summary of previous work in field)

Division of topic into categories such as observations and results

Conclusions

Recommendations

Back section:

References

Bibliography

Appendixes

Be aware of logical divisions in the material, and keep data within the appropriate category. Procedural information goes in the procedural section; results go in the results section. Mixing sections of reports creates both logical and organizational problems for readers.

**A Section-by-
Section Look
at a Report
on Thermal
Insulation**

In most first-year engineering programs, students write weekly reports documenting their experiments, especially during the first course.

In this example, we're going to look at how several teams of students handled each part of the reports they wrote during their first semester in a first-year engineering class.

In this instance, the students were reporting on a thermal insulation competition—a competition in which each team of students had to design and build a container that would minimize the amount of heat lost by a hot egg. The team with the least heat lost from its egg over 10 minutes would win the competition.

Each team was given materials (foam chips, plastic wrap, tape, cardboard, aluminum foil) and a digital thermometer with a thermocouple and wire connectors.

The materials could be cut, drilled, and arranged in any way inside the plastic container supplied. No external heat sources could be used.

The container had to be at room temperature; it also had to be designed so that it would open to accept the egg once the egg had been heated to 150° F. The digital thermometer had to be connected to the surface of the egg.

All teams were required to take notes throughout the experiment.

- They recorded the reasons for their design in their laboratory notebooks.
- They sketched the container they intended to build.
- They wrote a group report documenting the design, construction, and testing of the container.

You are going to see examples from these team reports, with comments on the writing next to each example. Here are the parts of the reports that are shown:

1. *Title page:* A before-and-after version is shown, first as the title page was originally written, then as it was revised.

2. *Abstract:* Original and revised versions are shown.

3. *Introduction:* Two examples of introductions are shown in their original and revised forms. You can see that the authors take different approaches, but that both approaches are effective.

4. *Procedure:* In one example, the procedural steps are listed; in the other, the procedure is given as a continuous narrative. Both approaches have their advantages:

> *The listing pattern* is easy for others to follow, but takes up a lot of space.
>
> *The continuous narrative* is succinct.

5. *Data/observations:* In the first example, the team was successful. In the second example, the team failed to win the competition, but they were able to explain their puzzling results clearly.

6. *Discussion/conclusions:* The successful and unsuccessful teams both explain their results in a satisfactory way.

Example 1   Title page: Original

Laboratory 10:
Thermal Insulation Competition
Name:
Richard Chen
Date: 12/9/97

[omitted names of partners]
[The date could be interpreted as either September 12 or December 9.]

Example 2   Title page: Revised

Laboratory 10:
Thermal Insulation Competition
Team Members:
Richard Chen
Susan James
Gary Nguyen
Elizabeth Ross
Date:
December 9, 1997
Class:
EG 101, Section D, Bench B

[All partners' names are included.]

[The date is clarified.]

[Note author's use of boldface to show the divisions or main sections of the title page.]

Example 3   Abstract: Original version

Abstract

The objective of this experiment was to design, build, and test a container that would reduce the heat lost by an egg heated to 150° F.

[Sometimes laboratory instructors will let you substitute a statement of the objective for a full abstract. In this example, though, students were asked to write a full abstract. This team's abstract has the objective of the experiment, but does not have a summary of the procedure, results, and conclusions. A good abstract includes what you found out (the results or main findings) and what the findings mean (the conclusions and recommendations).]

Example 4   Abstract: Revised version

Abstract

The objective of this experiment was to design, build, and test a container that would reduce the heat lost by an egg initially heated to 150° F.

[objective]

We designed a container with an inner double wrapping of plastic wrap and an outer layer of poly fill.

[procedure]

Total heat loss during the test interval was 10.3 degrees. The decrease in heat loss was steady over the 10 minutes.

[results]

Thus, the insulation proved to be effective;

[conclusion]

however, it might be further improved by placing aluminum foil around the egg after the two layers of plastic wrap.

[recommendation]

Example 5   A revised abstract

Abstract

In this experiment we had to design and build a container that would effectively insulate a hot egg.

[objective]

Our container consisted of several layers of cotton taped around the egg.

[procedure]

During the 10-minute measurement interval, the temperature of our egg fluctuated until it reached 143.1° F, after which it steadily declined until it was 142.3° F.

[results]

The thermocouple wires were not in proper contact with the egg, so the measurements were erratic.

[conclusion]

Example 6   An introduction: Original version

Introduction

This report outlines the design strategy, actual design, and testing of the container and the improvements needed for better design. The results are shown in graphical form. The rules of the competition are also outlined.

[The introduction should state the problem, background, or issue, followed by the significance of the issue. A good way to end the introduction is to give a roadmap or summary of the contents that follow. Here the authors have summarized the objective and some of the contents of the report, but have omitted the problem or background statement.]

Example 7 An introduction: Revised version

Introduction

Insulation is a material that protects against cold, heat, sound, or electricity. Thermal insulation is insulation related specifically to heat (from *therme,* Greek for *heat*). According to the *World Book Encyclopedia,* several layers of insulation provide greater protection than one thick layer with the same total weight. This is due to the insulating effect of the air between layers.

[The opening paragraphs of the introduction give the background and the nature of the problem addressed.]

The following report describes our entry into a competition to design a thermal insulation for a hot egg. The rules of the competition were that only the materials supplied in the class might be used, but these might be cut, drilled, or arranged as needed, provided all materials remained within the plastic container; no external heat sources might be used; the container must be at room temperature, and the thermocouple must remain in constant contact with the egg after the container was closed.

This report outlines the design and testing of the container we built to maximize the insulating effect of air between layers. It concludes with suggestions of improvements for a better design in the future.

[This is a "roadmap"—it tells what is coming up in the report. The roadmap is an effective way to end an introduction, for it lets the reader know the organization and highlights of the document that follows. Introductions needn't be lengthy, but they do have to give the reader a summary of the problem, background, or issue, and information about how the sections that follow the introduction are organized.]

Example 8   A revised introduction

Introduction

Thermal energy or heat is transferred from one place to another by three processes: convection, conduction, and radiation. In conduction, heat is transferred by interactions of the molecules of the objects in contact with one another. In convection, heat is transported by direct mass transport, such as when warm air rises because of its lower density. In radiation, energy (heat) is emitted by bodies in the form of electromagnetic radiation and is absorbed by other bodies.

[This gives the background of the problem.]

In this report, we will discuss how we used these properties of heat transfer to come up with a design for our thermal insulator.

[roadmap]

Example 9   A procedure in listing form

Procedure

1. The egg was boiled, and then placed immediately in the container.

2. The egg was centered in the box, so that its sides did not touch the sides of the box.

3. The thermocouple from the digital thermometer was attached to the boiled egg.

4. The egg was wrapped first with cotton and then with a layer of plastic. It was then taped to the bottom of the container and wrapped a second time with plastic.

5. Poly fill was added to insulate the area between the egg and the walls of the container. (See Figure 1–1.)

6. The testing was conducted at 30-second intervals over 10 minutes; however, testing did not commence until the egg reached 150° F.

[Here the authors use passive voice for the procedure. Note that the authors are telling what they actually did, rather than re-copying the printed steps in the procedure for the experiment.]

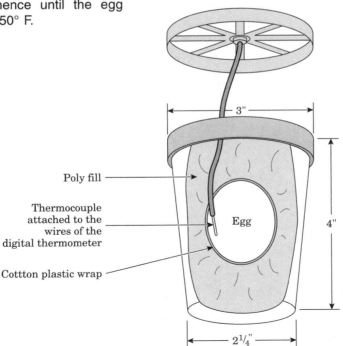

Figure 1–1
Thermal insulation report

Poly fill

Thermocouple attached to the wires of the digital thermometer

Cottton plastic wrap

3"

Egg

4"

2¼"

Example 10 A procedure in continuous narrative form

Procedure

We used cotton as the basic insulation, cutting off a piece to fit into the foam cup and then cutting a second, thinner piece of cotton of the same size. We taped the two layers of cotton together and stuffed them in the foam cup. (See Figure 1–2.) Then we cut a third piece of cotton the size of the lid and held it in reserve. When the egg was heated, we put the thermocouple wires into the small hole in the middle of the lid and then through the third piece of cotton shaped to go beneath the lid. We taped the thermocouple wire to the egg, added the cotton cut to fit the lid, added the lid, and taped it down. We took the temperature every 30 seconds for 15 minutes and recorded the data on the Excel worksheet.

[These authors use active voice for the procedure.]

Figure 1–2
Thermal insulation report

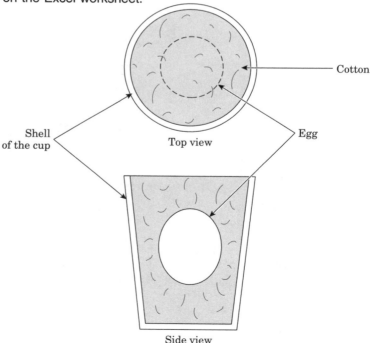

Example 11   A data/observations section

Data/Observations

During the design and testing of the container, the team realized that some of the materials provided were better insulators than others. For instance, the plastic wrap was preferable to foam chips.

The team also realized that the egg had to be placed near the center of the cup, for if it was touching the sides of the cup, heat would easily be released.

The results on our data sheet* show that the temperature dropped approximately 10° from its starting temperature of 150° F. This drop was quite steady over the tested interval.

*Data sheet not shown in this example.

[Note that the authors use the words the team *and its accompanying pronoun,* we. *This enables them to cast the bulk of their observations in the active voice.]*

Example 12 A data/observations section

Data/Observations

The initial temperature of the egg in the container was 130.0° F. The temperature increased from this point until it reached a maximum of 152.0° F. The temperature then fluctuated, decreasing and increasing until it reached 143.1° F, after which it steadily decreased. (See Table 1–1). When we examined the cup closely, we saw that a part of the cup had been pushed in when we were putting on the lid, and that the lid had therefore not covered the cup tightly. When we opened the cup after the experiment, we saw that the thermocouple wires did not have good contact with the egg.

[Note the integration of the table into the narrative. This is an effective technique, for reports are usually easier to read when the figures and tables are as close as possible to first reference in the narrative. An alternative is to place the table at the end of the report as an attachment.]

Table 1–1 Lab 10 data

Time (sec.)	Temp (° F)
0	152.0
30	148.4
60	146.0
90	149.4
120	149.7
150	138.0
180	138.8
210	140.7
240	137.6
270	138.9
300	137.8
330	140.1
360	140.0
390	138.6
420	138.3
450	142.3
480	142.8
510	143.1
540	143.0
570	142.7
600	142.3
630	142.0
660	141.6
690	141.1
720	140.9
750	140.8
780	140.5
810	140.0
840	139.6
870	139.8
900	140.5

Example 13   A discussion/conclusions section

Discussion/Conclusions

Our design was a fairly good example of thermal insulation. Most important was the choice of materials, for they were major factors in determining whether the egg could retain as much heat as possible. Plastic wrap turned out to be the best material to contain the air molecules, followed by the poly fill to insulate the outer space.

Were we to rebuild our insulator cup, we would place aluminum foil around the egg after the two layers of plastic wrap. Then the poly fill would be placed in the rest of the container.

[The authors draw their conclusion.]

[The authors make a recommendation.]

Example 14   A discussion/conclusion section

Discussion/Conclusion

We tried to reduce conduction and convection in our design. To this end, we decided not to use aluminum foil because it was a good conductor and therefore would take heat away from the egg if it touched the egg. Instead, we used cotton because it does not conduct heat well. We chose multiple layers of cotton because layers permit less convection. We also put tape around the layers of cotton to keep the heat from escaping.

[The authors explicitly link the discussion to their statement of the problem in the introduction.]

Our egg lost a total of 11.5° F in 15 minutes. When we plotted the temperature-vs.-time graph (Figure 1–3), the results were not a straight line. This occurred because the thermocouple wires did not have good contact with the egg. We received irregular temperature readings that decreased and then increased.

[The authors explain experimental problems and inconsistencies in measurement.]

Figure 1–3
Temp vs. time graph

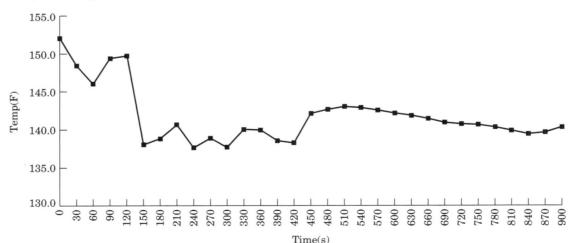

Were we to rebuild the container, we would think more about radiation.

The winning design in our class suggested an idea for a way to use aluminum effectively. Were we to redo the experiment, we would put aluminum around the inside of the cup and the inside of the lid. Although aluminum is mainly a conductor, it is also a good radiator and therefore it might radiate all the heat that comes toward it back to the egg. Another way to improve the design might be to put the thermocouple wires into the container and then stuff the egg over the wires.

[The authors continue to link the conclusion to the issue they raised in the introduction.]

[The authors discuss application of this experiment to the future.]

Coherence in Longer Reports

2

Outline

The sections of a report should flow logically from one another—the reader of your report should be able to follow the relationship of the introduction to the procedure, the relationship of the procedure to the results, and the relationship of the results to the discussion. Each section must be linked logically to the next.

To do this effectively, you must connect the objectives in your introduction to what you say in the procedure, results, and discussion. This connection can't be tacit or understood—it has to be *explicit*; that is, you must *use the words of the narrative to link your objectives to your procedure and findings*.

In this way, you can test to make sure one point is logically related to the next. Ask yourself, Is my objective connected to what I've found out? Have I explained any inconsistencies in the results in relation to my objective? Have I connected my findings to my original statement of the problem?

When you are done, the argument should be coherent—the report should make one central point or set of points, and those points should be illustrated in each section of the report, which together constitute a whole. If the report is coherent, the reader will be able to see the logical connections within the argument you are making.

The following report was written by a student learning about the functions of the oscilloscope. The experiment introduced basic controls and operations of the oscilloscope, including ac and dc coupling modes.

As you will see, the report is not coherent—the logical connections between the sections of the report are not established.

Example 1   Original version of a report on the functions of the oscilloscope
Report 10:   The Oscilloscope

[The abstract or statement of objective is missing; therefore, the reader has no overview.]

Introduction

The oscilloscope is a voltmeter that is able to display measured values in graphical form. The objective of this experiment was to become familiar with the operation of the oscilloscope by performing a series of measurements designed to illustrate the basic functions of the major oscilloscope controls. The experiment was broken into three major parts.

[What are the three major parts?]

Experimental Work

The oscilloscope is used to observe the sine wave output of the function generator. The voltage is set to 2 V rms and the frequency was set to 1000 Hz. Both were then checked with the oscilloscope. Various controls are adjusted to see the impact on the wave-form.

The oscilloscope allows the user to set the trigger to be an internal or external source. For the experiment, the trigger was set to Line. I changed the frequency of the function generator, and observed where the wave-form was the least dynamic. This was checked at several frequencies, and then compared to what the frequency value should be, a multiple of the trigger frequency.

I observed the ramifications of both coupling modes (ac and dc) with a square-wave input.

Results and Conclusions

I noted that the settings that were given yielded two cycles on the oscilloscope, which is what was expected because the period of the sine wave was set to 1 ms. The horizontal axis of the oscilloscope was set to .2 ms per division, and so with 10 divisions there is just enough space to show two complete wave-forms.

To determine the accuracy of the oscilloscope I compared the peak-to-peak voltage and converted it to an RMS value. This is then compared with the DMM.

The rms value is calculated by

$$V_{rms} = V_p / \sqrt{2} \qquad (1)$$

[Note the way the author gives the procedure in the past tense sometimes and in the present sometimes: "The voltage is set . . . the frequency was set."]

[What is the relationship of this information to the introduction? The author has not connected this section to the preceding one.]

[Note that abbreviations like RMS and DMM are not defined, and that the appearances of ac, dc, RMS, and DMM are inconsistent, sometimes all capitals, and sometimes lower case.]

The value from the oscilloscope is 2.03 V, whereas the DMM read 2.05 V. The two are obviously very close to being equal.

The values of the frequencies read off the function generator are listed in Table 2–1. Upon inspection of the table it can be said that the function generator is slightly inaccurate.

Table 2–1I

Freq. (signal)	30	60	90
120	180	240	300
(Hz)			
Freq. (trigger)	28	59	89
118	182	242	297
(Hz)			

The coupling modes of the oscilloscope are seen to be both an advantage and a detriment. The dc mode allows all signals to pass through to the oscilloscope screen. This is useful because then there are no "surprises" (i.e., all voltages are seen).

The AC mode on the other hand blocks any dc signal, which can be lethal.

[The meaning of "lethal"—that is, that the dc signal could damage the oscilloscope—is not clear; the author needs to use a more precise word.]

Additionally, in the ac mode we observe a decay in the wave form as the coupling capacitance forms an RC circuit.

[Which wave form is the author discussing? The square wave?]
[What is the relationship of the information in this section to the introduction and procedure? Are the results consistent with the objectives? Are inconsistencies explained? We can't tell, because there is no link between this information and any other section of the report.]

If you had difficulty following the report on the oscilloscope, it might be because of the way the report is organized.

- *In the introduction,* the author needs to indicate the subject of each part of the experiment, so that the reader can see how the report is divided, and then follow the division in the procedure and discussion that follow. This experiment has three parts. Each part needs to be identified.
- *In the experimental section,* the author needs to connect the procedure to objectives or parts that must be stated in the introduction.
- *In the discussion section,* the author needs to connect the conclusions to the objectives or parts that must be stated in the introduction.

Here is a revised version of the report that is far more cohesive. The writer has clarified the relationship of the parts of the report to the central argument, making sure that each section follows logically from the original objectives of the experiment. The writer has also added a statement of objective at the beginning.

Example 2 Revised version of a report on the functions of the oscilloscope

Report 10: The Oscilloscope

Objective and Scope

The oscilloscope is a useful laboratory instrument for measuring the properties of periodic wave forms. This experiment introduces basic controls and operations of the oscilloscope, including advantages and disadvantages of ac and dc coupling modes.

[The author gives an abbreviated version of an abstract—in this case, a statement of objective and scope. This works well to give an overview for the subject.]

Introduction

The oscilloscope is a voltmeter that is able to display measured values in graphical form. The objective of this experiment is to become familiar with the operation of the oscilloscope by performing a series of measurements designed to illustrate the basic function of the major oscilloscope controls.

The experiment is broken into three major parts, each part covering a different aspect of the oscilloscope:

1. The connection of a function generator directly to the oscilloscope to obtain and measure an image.

2. A test of the accuracy of the frequency of the signal generator using the line triggering mode.

3. An observation of the advantages and disadvantages of two input coupling modes of the oscilloscope.

Experimental Work

A function generator is an electronic device that can produce various voltage waves, including a sine wave. In the first part of the experiment, a function generator was connected directly to the oscilloscope to obtain an image on the scope. Afterwards, the peak-to-peak voltage of the image was measured and converted to rms (root mean square) voltage to see if the calculated rms voltage agreed with the digital multimeter (DMM) reading.

In the experiment, the function generator was set to generate a 1000 Hz sine wave with an amplitude of 2 V rms; then the DMM was used to determine the voltage output of the generator more accurately. After the signal was measured with the DMM, it was confirmed with the oscilloscope, which measured the peak-to-peak voltage from the image of the sine wave on the oscilloscope screen. The appearance of the wave form was observed with the oscilloscope set at 0.2 ms/dir.

[All sections of the report will flow logically from this division. The roadmap shows the structure of the report that will follow.]

[Procedure for Part 1 of the experiment: The writer tells what was done, explicitly linking this information to the objective for Part I given in the introduction.]

The second part of the experiment tested the accuracy of the frequency of the sine waves generated by the signal generator. To do this, the trigger was set to Line, which is 60 Hz. The frequency of the function generator was then changed to observe the settings for which one could observe a stationary image. Afterwards, a short table comparing actual frequencies with the dial setting on the generator was prepared.

[Procedure for Part 2 of the experiment: The writer links this procedure to the objective given in the introduction for Part 2. The table will be in the discussion section. Notice that past tense is used throughout to give the procedure.]

In the third part of the experiment, the advantages and disadvantages of the two input modes of the oscilloscope were compared: dc and ac coupling modes. Once a sine wave was displayed on the oscilloscope, the dc offset of the function generator was varied. That added a constant voltage to the sine wave. The change in the image using dc-v.-ac coupling modes was then observed. A square wave was then substituted for a sine wave, and the comparison of dc and ac made again.

[Procedure for Part 3 of the experiment.]

Discussion and Conclusions

In Part 1—the connection of a function generator directly to the oscilloscope to obtain an image—the settings that were given yielded two cycles on the oscilloscope. This was expected because the period of the sine wave was set to 1 ms. (The period is the reciprocal of the frequency, therefore, as the frequency was 1000 Hz, 1/1000 Hz = 1 ms.) The horizontal axis of the oscilloscope was set to .2 ms per division, and so with 10 divisions there was just enough space to show two complete wave forms.

[The author links the discussion explicitly to the introduction.]

Measuring the point-to-point voltage of the image and converting it to rms voltage using the equation given

$$V_{rms} = V_p/\sqrt{2} \qquad (1)$$

it was possible to see if the calculated rms voltage agreed with the DMM reading. The value from the oscilloscope was 2.03 V; the DMM read 2.05 V. The two were close to equal.

[The author gives his conclusion for Part 1 of the experiment.]

Part 2 was a test of the accuracy of the frequency of the signal generator. The frequency of the function generator was changed until a stationary image was observed. The settings that resulted in the stationary image were whole-number multiples of 60/2 or 30 Hz. The table then prepared (see Table I) shows actual frequencies in comparison with the dial setting on the generator. Table **2–1** shows that the function generator was slightly inaccurate.

[The author gives conclusions for Part 2 of the experiment.]

Table 2–1

Freq. (signal)	30	60	90
120	180	240	300
(Hz)			
Freq. (trigger)	28	59	89
118	182	242	297
(Hz)			

In Part 3, it became clear that the coupling modes of the oscilloscope offered both advantages and detriments. The dc mode allows all signals to pass through to the oscilloscope screen. This is useful because then there are no "surprises" (i.e., all voltages are seen). In ac mode, the sine wave stays centered at all times. The ac mode, on the other hand, blocks any dc signal, which can result in damage to the oscillo-

[The author gives conclusions for Part 3.]

scope. Additionally, in the ac mode a decay in the square wave form is observed as the coupling capacitance forms an RC circuit. This is evident in the wave forms at the lower frequencies, which are also blocked by the capacitance.

Sometimes in first-year engineering classes, and often in second-, third-, and fourth-year engineering classes, students must write long reports. The reports are often based on a research problem, a design issue, or a combination of research and design.

The following report was written by an undergraduate. It combines a research problem with design work.

The organization of the report is coherent, and the writing is very clear.

After you read each section of the report, note the comments in the margin explaining some of the techniques the author used.

Example 3 Fluorescence microscopy of a levitated aerosol particle

Abstract

An aerosol particle fluorescence microscope (APFM) is described for characterizing impurity chromophores within an aerosol particle. The particle is isolated by electrostatic levitation and electrodynamic trapping. Micrographs of octadecyl rhodamine B (ODRB) in glycerol are obtained which show that the fluor is a surfactant. By analyzing images taken through a polarizer, using a model built on molecular optics, the orientation of the emission moment was ascertained. This assignment and rudimentary physical chemistry are used to describe the orientation of ODRB on the particle surface. The APFM is expected to find a wide range of applications in fields such as environmental and medical research.

[The abstract answers five basic questions: What did he do? Why did he do it? How did he do it? What did he find out? What do these findings signify?]

Introduction

Microparticles in air, such as biological spores or other aerosol particles, partake in biological reproduction and in the dissemination of disease [1], provide small "test tubes" for brewing acid rain, and are a subject of continual environmental monitoring. [2] Although such particles are commonly investigated by collecting the particles on filter paper for spectrochemical analyses, this method can corrupt the particles in several ways. Contact can easily lead to chemical contamination, physical distortion, and charge transfer. However, it should be possible in principle to obtain physical and chemical information using spectrally resolved microphotographs of an individual aerosol particle while isolated through levitation and trapping techniques. [3]

In our laboratory, we have introduced a means for investigating a single aerosol particle "in situ," through microphotography on a levitated particle. [4] In addition to contributing to the construction and design of the microscope, our work has expanded into fluorescence microphotography. By spectrally resolving microphotographs of levitated microdroplets containing fluorescent molecules, it is possible to determine if the molecules are surfactants (molecules localized to the particle surface). In addition, by analyzing polarization components in these images we have been able to estimate the surface orientation of surfactant fluorophores.

[Author provides a statement of the problem or issue, and gives references to back up the statement of the problem. (The bracketed numbers refer to citations for related literature. These citations appear at the end of the report.) Note use of present tense.]

[Note the definition of the term surfactant in parentheses. Note the use of present tense.]

In what follows we describe our aerosol particle fluorescence microscope (APFM), discuss the preparation of individual particles, present results on the fluorescence microphotography of surfactant chromophores, and discuss these results in terms of the physics of fluorescence and the physical chemistry of molecules at a liquid's surface.

[The author provides a "roadmap" of the coming discussion; that is, he tells the readers the forthcoming organization of the report. Note that all unfamiliar abbreviations are defined on first use. Note that all the terminology is consistent—for instance, no term is shown in upper case on one page and then in lower case on the next page.]

Method

[The author divides the following section into three parts: Equipment, Materials, and Procedure. This allows the reader to see the basic division of the section.]

Equipment

A. The Aerosol Particle Fluorescence Microscope

The aerosol particle microscope (APM) consists of an optical microscope that views a trapped aerosol particle. It is the first of its kind, and was designed and constructed in its current form by myself and others in the summer of 1993. Originally it was used to test theory associated with elastic scattering. [4] In its current form as an aerosol particle fluorescence microscope (APFM), it is affixed with optical filters and polarizers for recording images in inelastic fluorescence scattering. A more detailed description follows.

[Note that the author writes out the new terms aerosol particle microscope *and* aerosol particle fluorescence microscope *in full the first time he uses them. Then he follows with their abbreviations enclosed in parentheses. In any future uses of the terms in the paper, he can simply use the abbreviations.]*

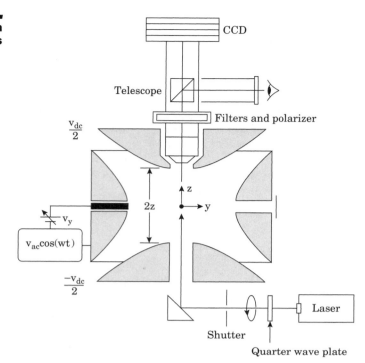

Figure 2–1
Aerosol particle
fluorescence microscope

Figure 2–1 shows the aerosol particle fluorescence microscope (APFM). The microscope and associated apparatus consist of an electrodynamic levitator trap (ELT, with a characteristic dimension from the center to the top electrode z_o of 4.5 mm) equipped with lateral-centering electrodes, a home-made microscope, and a cooled integrating CCD camera. Enclosed within the body of the microscope is an optical filter and a rotating polarizer. The potential near the center of the trap is the sum of both the ac and dc parts, with the dc electric field used to balance the weight of the particle and the ac field used in creating alternating gradient forces for trapping. [5,6] In addition, the micro-

[If the equipment you are using is standard, giving the manufacturer and model number is sufficient. In this case, however, the team built the equipment, so it must be described.]

scope body contains a beam-splitter that allows for simultaneous viewing and imaging of the particle. An argon ion laser was used to excite the doped microparticles. To remove any effects of the laser's polarization, the beam was converted from a linear polarized beam to a circular polarized beam using a quarter wave plate. Bi-directional ports allowed for excitation of the particles from beneath and from the side.

B. Picopipettes for Preparation of Individual Particles

Particles are generated using a device similar in construction to the printing industry's ink jet. However, the device developed at our lab acts more like a pipette than an ink jet. This device can accurately deliver picoliter quantities of solution (see "Picopipette" in Fig. 2–2); this is six orders of magnitude below the current state of the art in pipettes. Solution for the particle is sucked into a glass tip (orifice approximately 30 μ in diameter).

[Note how figure and narrative work together to explain this equipment adapted by the author for the project.]

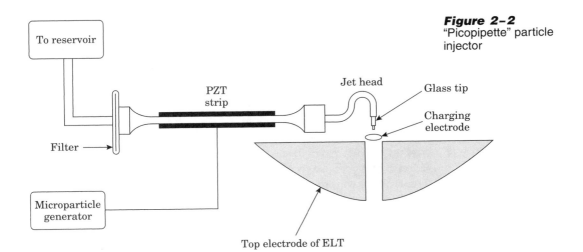

Figure 2–2
"Picopipette" particle injector

By applying a voltage pulse to piezoelectric strips in the jet's body, a small droplet (approximately 20 μ radius) is squeezed out from the orifice at the end of the tip. The particles are inductively charged as they are emitted by generating an electric field at the orifice. This is accomplished by placing an electrified washer in front of the glass tip.

Materials

Two dyes know as Dil and ODRB were used in the particles for fluorescent imaging. From their structure, both were likely to be surface active (surfactant) with emission bands in the visible region. Surfactant molecules contain both hydrophobic and hydrophilic portions that enable the molecules to align at the interface of a polar liquid and air. The hydrophilic portion of the molecule remains in the polar solvent while the nonpolar portions, which are hydrophobic, are pushed into the air. The structure of each of these dyes is shown in Figure 2–3.

[Note how the author coordinates the narrative with the illustrations, using a citation such as "See Figure" the first time he refers to each figure.]

Procedure

Both dyes were initially dissolved in methanol solution and then mixed with glycerol to the concentrations (in glycerol) of 8.6 l0^{-5}M for Dil and 8.6 10^{-5}M for ORDB. Once the desired concentration was obtained, the solution was diluted with methanol to a ratio of 1:2 by volume of glycerol to methanol. The dilution with methanol was needed to reduce the viscosity of the solution to facilitate droplet ejection from the picopipette.

[The author uses continuous narrative, past tense, and passive voice.]

Dil: 1,1'-dioctadecyl-3,3,3',3'-tetramethylindocarbocyanine perchlorate

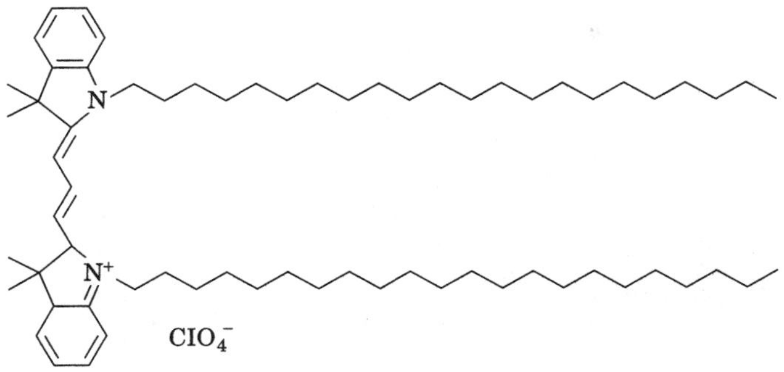

ODRB: octadecyl rhodamine B, chloride salt

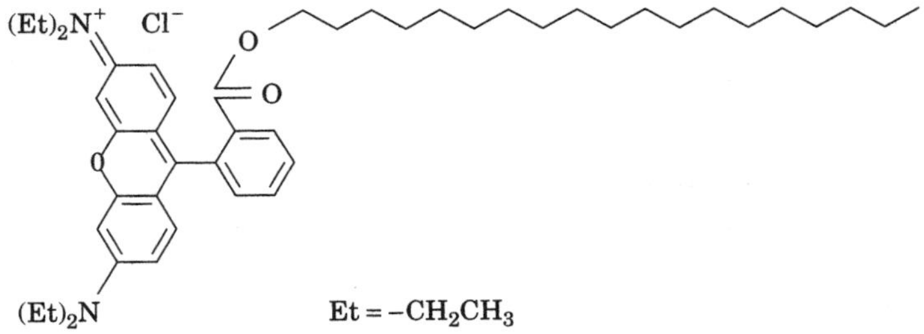

$Et = -CH_2CH_3$

Figure 2–3
Structure of molecules used in the fluorescent imaging experiments

Once captured and balanced in the electrodynamic trap, the particle was irradiated from below with a circular polarized beam from an argon ion laser (λmax = 488 nm). Since the laser beam was directed toward the detector, the relatively weak fluorescence from the particle was easily overwhelmed by the intense laser beam. This problem was overcome by introducing appropriate optical filters into the microscope to block the laser and transmit the fluorescence from the particle.

Results

Figure 2–4 shows the luminescence from a glycerol/ODRB particle. It is apparent that there are two prominent high-intensity regions: one at the center

[The author uses the narrative to highlight points readers will need for the discussion section.]

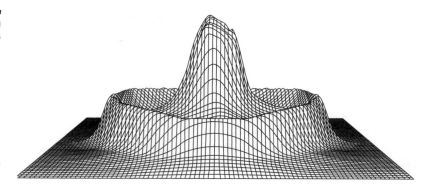

Figure 2–4
Topograph 1

and the other at a rim near the edge. Notably, the rim appears to be almost constant in intensity as one proceeds along the circumference. The region in the center is essentially uniform out to about 25% of the radius and then falls abruptly. Images taken on fluors without the aliphatic tails show no outer rim, although there is still intense luminescence at the center. We therefore conjecture that the outer rim is associated with surfactant molecules. These molecules are expected to cover the entire sphere; however, the prominent rim may be understood by mathematically projecting a uniformly surface-coated sphere onto a plane. Near the rim, molecules line up behind one another and the projected density goes through an extremum. The topograph (Figure 2–4) of this image shows the actual intensities and is consistent with our previous discussion.

In Figure 2–5, we clearly see that the emission from the

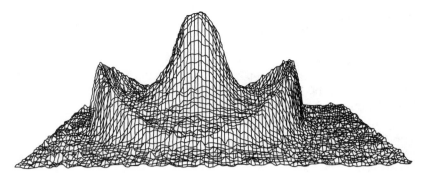

Figure 2–5
Topograph 2

edge of the particle is polarized. It should be pointed out that no particular polarization state (i.e., x or y) is impressed on the surface by the incident radiation, since the laser beam is circularly polarized. Consequently, the effect seen in Figure 2–5 is due entirely to an emission anisotropy. The degree of this effect is shown in Figure 2–5. This figure shows a topograph of intensity versus position in the x–y plane. Note that the polarizer appears to extinguish the luminescence from the rim along the y-axis, although the rim is prominent along the other axis. Similar effects were seen with the other fluor.

Discussion of Results

Here we describe the polarized intensity from the rim using a simple molecular-electrodynamic model. We will see that in the process, information concerning the molecular orientation is revealed.

Since the molecules on the

surface are excited by an incident plane wave that is circularly polarized and directed along the z-axis, the z-axis is an axis of symmetry in the electromagnetic problem, the problem of determining the field at the surface of the sphere. Therefore, all points on the edge receive the same intensity. This uniform intensity along with the statistical effect of averaging over molecular orientation ϕ_m at a given position θ produces a uniform rim of fluorescence as seen in the data (Figure 2−4). However, the fluorescence itself is polarized because of the vector nature of emission and the tendency for molecules to align at the surface. Using this presumed alignment and other aspects associated with symmetry, it is possible to explain the anisotropy observed in the analyzed image (Figure 2−5).

The image in Figure 2−5 may be understood in terms of the schematic diagram shown in Figure 2−6. Here we assume the emission moment μ of an emitting molecule is oriented at angle (θ_m, ϕ_m). Its "global" position is described by the spherical polar coordinates a, θ, ϕ, where a is the radius of the sphere, θ is the polar angle, and ϕ is the azimuthal angle. The emission moment may be characterized by its components in the "local" coordinate system

$$\mu = \mu[\cos(\theta_m)k_m + \sin(\theta_m)\cos(\phi_m)i_m + \sin(\theta_m)\sin(\phi_m)j_m] \qquad (1)$$

where i_m, j_m, and k_m are a "local" Cartesian set of unit vectors with k_m perpendicular to

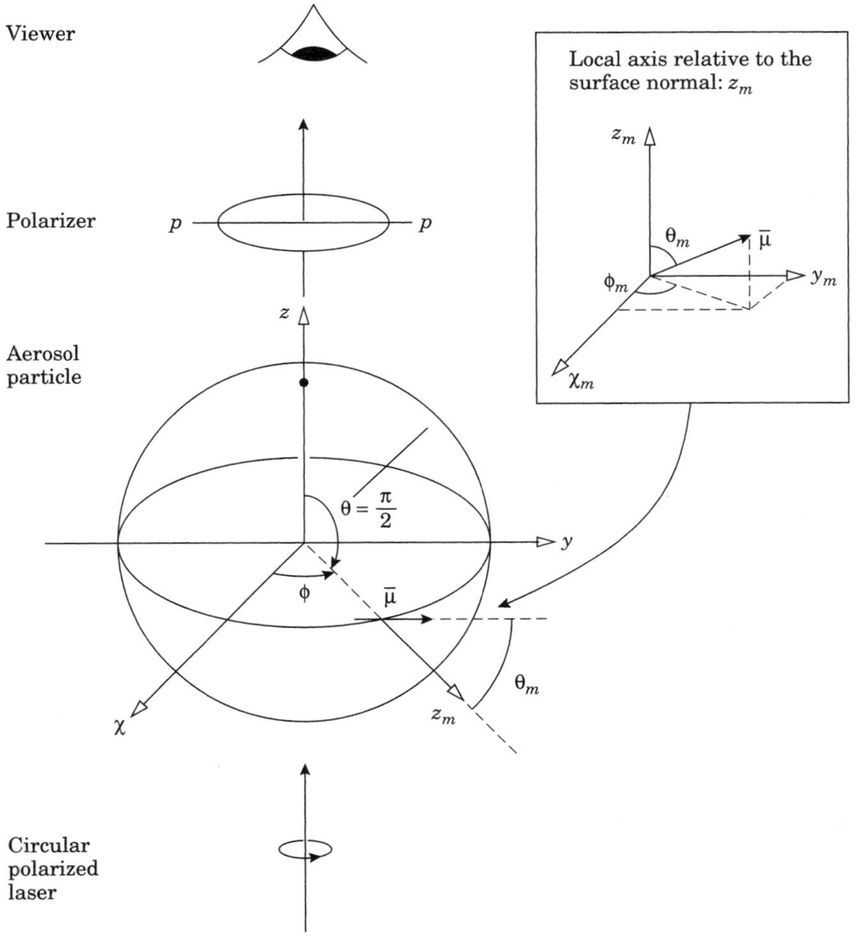

Figure 2–6
Molecular emission
moment on surface of
sphere

the surface. In our experiment, the laser beam is directed in the positive "global" z direction, the microscope views in the $-z$ direction, and the fluorescent sources at the edge are positioned at a "global" polar angle $\theta \simeq \pi/2$. Consequently, we confine our interest to these sources. An optically excited molecule can be considered to act as an oscillating dipole. Such a dipole radiates with an emission field which is proportional to the transition moment μ (the strength of the oscillating dipole moment)[7].

The major influence on the polarization properties of the emitted light is contained in the orientation of the dipole. At a detector, which is very far along the z-axis (i.e., $z/a \gg 1$), the principal transition moment components that are responsible for the associated image are those that are perpendicular to z (i.e., the x_m and y_m components in Figure 2–6). Thus, we can write out the scattered field from the emitter in Fig. 2–6 as

$$E \propto \mu[a_{per}\cos(\theta_m)k_m + a_{par}\sin(\theta_m)\sin(\phi_m)j_m] \qquad (2)$$

where a_{per} and a_{par} take account for any bias in emission strength associated with perpendicular or parallel components, respectively. Such constants are not necessary for a free dipole; however, just as interaction with the sphere causes a structural break in symmetry leading to alignment, it also is expected to alter the electromagnetic response. Now we are in a position to understand the angular intensity dependence measured in Figure 2–5.

The intensity at the image plane associated with a given dipole can be obtained by introducing a polarizer in the optical path between the particle and its image. If the polarizer is oriented along the "global" y-axis, then the intensity transmitted, I, will involve the projection of **E** on a unit vector along the y-axis (j). Specifically using Equation 2,

$$I \propto |\mathbf{E} \cdot \mathbf{j}|^2 \propto \mu^2[a_{per}\cos(\theta_m) (\mathbf{k}_m \cdot \mathbf{j}) + a_{par}\sin(\theta_m)\sin(\phi_m) (\mathbf{j}_m \cdot \mathbf{j})]^2 \qquad (3a)$$

The products $(\mathbf{k}_m \cdot \mathbf{j})$ and $(\mathbf{j}_m \cdot \mathbf{j})$ at $\theta = \pi/2$ are $\sin(\phi)$ and $\cos(\theta)$, respectively, which allows Equation 3 to be evaluated as

$$I \propto \mu^2(a_{per})^2\{[\cos(\theta_m)\sin(\phi)]^2 + (a_{par}/a_{per})^2[\sin(\theta_m)\sin(\phi_m)\cos(\phi)]^2\} \quad (3b)$$

Equation 3b pertains to a particular transition moment sitting on the edge at angle ϕ with orientation (θ_m,ϕ_m). However, our microscope does not view a point. Its resolution is limited to about one wavelength. In the interval of one wavelength ($\sim$5000 Å) there are many molecules. These molecules may be expected to be at a particular θ_m due to symmetry breaking at the surface, but the projection on the surface ϕ_m will be arbitrary. So it is appropriate to take an ensemble average of Equation 3b, in which we average over ϕ_m. By denoting the ensemble average by $\langle . . .\rangle$ and recognizing that $\langle\sin \phi_m\rangle = 0$, and $\langle[\sin \phi_m]^2\rangle = 1/2$, the ensemble averaged local intensity is

$$\langle I\phi; \theta_m)\rangle \propto \mu^2(a_{per})^2 \{[\cos(\theta_m)\sin(\phi)]^2 + (1/2)(a_{par}/a_{per})^2 [\sin(\theta_m)\cos(\phi)]^2\} \quad (4)$$

This equation may be written in a normalized form by adjusting the multiplicative constants so that $\langle I(0;\theta_m)\rangle = 1$. The normalized intensity is given by

$$\langle I(\phi)/I(0)\rangle = (1 - A)[\cos(\phi)]^2 - A \quad (5)$$

where $A = 2(a_{per}/a_{par})^2\cot^2(\theta_m)$.

On the basis of Equation 5, $\langle I(\phi)/I(0)\rangle$ should oscillate with a period of 180° and have minimum to maximum ratio = A. The period is in agreement with experiment. As shown in Figure 2−7, the minimum to maximum ratio from experiment is ≤1/50. If we assume that $(a_{per}/a_{par})^2 \simeq 1$, then for ODRM, $\theta_m \geq 85°$. Figure 2−7 shows a comparison between our experiment and theory as represented by Equation 5, for $\theta_m = 80°$ and 90°. It is clear that the transition moment is nearly tangent to the surface of the particle.

Since the transition moment of ORDB is known to lie in the plane of the three aromatic rings, our measurement for the direction of the transition moment is consistent with the plane of the rings being parallel with the plane of the particle's surface.

[The author gives a main conclusion.]

Conclusions

The results in Figure 2−7 show that it is possible to estimate the orientation of a surfactant molecule on a liquid's surface through long-term fluorescent imaging of doped aerosol

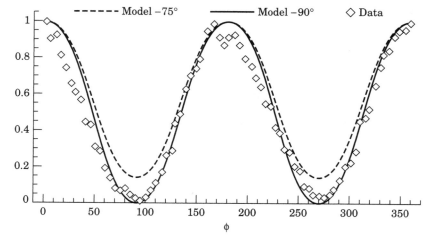

Figure 2−7
Comparison of
experimental angular
anisotropy with theory for
$\theta_m = 80°$ and 90°

particles in an electrodynamic trap.

In the past, information about molecules at a liquid gas phase boundary was limited to indirect measurements of quantities such as vapor pressure. However, since our system consisted of surfactant chromophores with polarized emission moments, we were able to exploit these properties to determine their surface orientation.

Our application of the APFM has just begun to explore its potential capabilities. This device and method should prove to be instrumental in environmental, biological, and medical research.

References

1. S. A. Satta, M. K. Ijaz, Spread of Viral Infections by Aerosols, Critical Reviews in Environmental Control **17,** no. 2, 89–131 (1987).

2. L. A. DeBlock, H. Van Malderren, R. E. Van Grieken, Individual Aerosol Particle Composition Variations in Air Masses Crossing the North Sea, Environmental Science & Technology, **28,** 1513–1550 (1994).

3. S. Arnold, L. M. Folan, and A. Korn, Optimal Imaging of a Charged Microparticle in a Paul Trap near STP: Stochastic Calculation and Experiment, J. Appl. Phys. **74,** 4291 (1993).

4. S. Arnold, S. Holler, J. H. Li, A. Serpenguzel, W. F. Aufferman, S. C. Hill, Aerosol Particle Microphotography and Glare Spot Absorption Spectroscopy Opt. Lett., **20,** 773 (1995).

5. H. G. Dehmelt, Radiofrequency Spectroscopy of Stored Ions I: Storage, Advan. Atomic and Mol. Physics **3,** 53 (1967).

6. E. H. Brandt, Levitation in Physics, Science, **243,** 349 (1989).

7. D. S. Kliger, J. W. Lewis, C. E. Randall, Polarized Light in Optics and Spectroscopy, p. 192, Harcourt Brace Jovanovich, Boston (1990).

Strategies: Ways to Use Teamwork, Laboratory Notebooks, and the Report Format to Help with the Writing Process

Outline

Many students have a favorite strategy when a writing assignment is due: They wait until the last minute, and then stay up all night. They are driven by the deadline—they count on the pressure to give them the last-minute energy to write.

Staying up all night may work occasionally when you are an undergraduate, but it is not a winning strategy for the workplace, which requires people who are reasonably well rested. It's also not the best strategy for a well-written document either at work or at school, for good writing requires revision, and revision means that the author has to look over the document several times to organize, shape, and word it effectively.

Revision works best when writers allow a little time to elapse between the time they write and the time they reread and revise their reports. A few hours away from the document gives the writer a fresh, critical perspective; the time break makes it easier for writers to see wording that could be improved and arguments that could be strengthened and better focused.

People who do a lot of writing have learned any number of techniques to help them finish writing jobs far enough in advance to allow time for revision.

They recognize that writing is difficult and that a strategy—one more sophisticated and practical than staying up all night—will help them move through the task more effectively.

Why Do People Develop Strategies to Handle the Writing Process?

Some strategies can help you with the writing process, so that you can build momentum well before the document is due, and use the extra time for focusing and revising your writing.

These strategies may help you get past the particularly tough parts in writing: assimilating data, getting started with composition, and avoiding roadblocks along the way.

Taking advantage of the way reports are organized—their division into parts, each with its specific functions—can be a big help in handling the writing process. Writing is always difficult—T. S. Eliot called it a "raid on the inarticulate, with shabby machinery, always deteriorating"—but an understanding of report format and the ways to use each section can actually ease the job of writing.

Here's a summary list of techniques students in first-year engineering programs say help them get through the process of writing:

How Can a Strategy Make Writing Easier?

- Brainstorming with colleagues or members of their team.
- Checking related research in the library, on the Internet, or through interviews with knowledgeable people.
- Using a laboratory notebook to sketch designs and keep track of experimental work in progress.
- Being realistic about time constraints.
- Guarding against distraction.

- Using the report format, with its fixed divisions of introduction, procedure, results, conclusions, and implications, to help them avoid roadblocks in the writing process.

How do these techniques work? Here's a look at each of them.

Brainstorming with Teammates

Talking with colleagues is called **brainstorming.** At work, teams often meet several times to hash out their ideas before they begin to write.

The process of talking eases the inherent difficulties of writing. That's why many people think that writing undertaken alone is far more stressful than writing collaboratively with colleagues.

Talking with your colleagues may be a good strategy not only at the beginning, but throughout the project, whenever you need help to think through a problem or get around a difficulty in your writing.

For example, in Chapter 1's case of the thermal insulation competition in which students designed a container for a hot egg, the teams regularly discussed various strategies for the design of the egg, coming up with many ideas for using the foam, aluminum foil, and cotton as they talked. The conferences gave them not only new ideas, but the impetus to keep going.

Looking at Related Literature

Science takes place not only in the laboratory, but in the library—or at the nearest computer with a connection to the Internet. People who do a lot of writing soon learn that before they write, they need to read the literature of the field. They may need to review the basic terminology of the problem. They may need to know who else has worked on the problem, or what researchers learned in the past, or how the new work adds to or differs from the previous work.

In the case of the thermal insulation competition, students researched the terminology of radiation and convection; they researched the meaning of the terms *insulation* and *heat transfer*, taking notes on what they learned. This broadened their understanding so that when they wrote the introduction, they had a better grasp of the problem they were addressing.

Where should you look? If you've no background at all in the subject, the first step is an overview of the sort provided by an *encyclopedia. Handbooks*, too, are traditional sources for general information. Third, there may be *textbooks* in the field with extensive reference lists. While the information may not be current, the references will provide an adequate beginning for background reading in the problem the report addresses. Encyclopedias, handbooks, and textbooks provide not only background information, but also citations that lead to other relevant publications. Because of their usefulness, they are a common starting point for beginning research on a topic.

The Internet and library search services can also lead you to *indexing* and *abstracting services* that will provide lists of articles within the topic. Indexes will give bibliographic citations, including title, author, and subject. Abstracts will provide synopses of articles and papers.

As your search broadens, you'll distinguish between *secondary sources* and *primary sources*. Secondary sources summarize and sometimes comment upon primary sources. For instance, a literature review or monograph that collects the past year's findings on advances in two-photon absorption spectroscopy is a secondary source.

Primary sources include refereed research journals, patents, and dissertations. While journal articles' introductions usually provide encapsulated reviews of relevant literature to establish the problem, the main function of a research report is to present data that are both new and significant. Therefore, while the research report may have useful information on secondary sources, it is a primary source.

Using a Laboratory Notebook

Memory is very fallible—it's easy to forget details of a project unless the details are written down. The best place to do notetaking for reports and other technical documentation is in a laboratory notebook.

Keeping a notebook will hone your eye, develop your descriptive powers, and add to your skill at ordering evidence and drawing inferences. The notebook occupies a well-earned cornerstone in scientific method. Chemists and civil engineers, physicists and doctors—all are enjoined in their professional training to use a notebook to preserve and protect data.

In the thermal insulation competition, students used their laboratory notebooks to write down their ideas for a good design. They wrote the reasons they preferred one material over another (for example, the use of cotton instead of aluminum foil) and were surprised when they reread their notes several days later. "I'd already forgotten that," one student commented. He found the notes very useful later when the time came to build the prototype and to write about the construction.

The laboratory notebook is an excellent place for preliminary sketches of the work you are going to undertake. Imagine dimensions and construction materials. Include this information in the sketch. The sketches will be invaluable when the time arrives to write.

Don't rely on your memory for details of the object. Write the details down before the image fades.

If possible, label the parts of the object. This information too may fade with time. Capture it before it evaporates.

Use the notebook throughout your projects to keep track of experimental work in progress. People familiar with the usefulness of notebooks keep them at hand when working on a problem, so that they can take notes on their work as their experiments progress. In the case of the insulating container, the team used the notebook first to record their progress building the container, and then to record the sequence of events as they tested the container to see how well it worked.

You may find that keeping a notebook ends up making report writing easier, for you'll have notes of the experiment, sketches of what you've done, and accurate, recorded details. The work of writing down the details and procedures as they occur will considerably lessen the job of writing the report itself—and your report will be more accurate, too.

You won't be the only person who has used a notebook to record and preserve your impressions. Many people before you have learned the advantages of notebooks. Thomas Edison left behind 3.5 million pages of work notes, among them 3,600 notebooks. Edison used his notebooks to sketch and to record observations. (He also doodled and occasionally practiced his calligraphy in the midst of sketching his inventions, as Figure 3–1 shows.) While developing the phonograph, for instance, Edison sketched a disc phonograph, made a list of parts to be designed, and wrote about applications of the phonograph (Figure 3–2).

Charles Darwin too was a famous keeper of notebooks. His *Journal and Remarks, 1832–1836, Vol. III*, of the *Voyage of the Beagle*, for instance, was based on 18 notebooks he kept. Here is his description of a new subdivision of the genus *Planari* (a type of worm), written in his notebooks after collecting the worm outside Rio de Janeiro:

> This like the last was caught in the forest crawling on soft decayed wood. It is quite a different species. Back snow white, edged each side by very fine lines of reddish-brown—also within are two other approximate ones

Two pages from Edison's notebooks. The inventor used his notebooks to sketch and to record his observations. (He also doodled and practiced his calligraphy.)

Figure 3–1   **Figure 3–2**

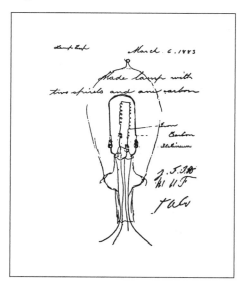
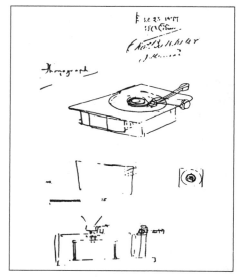

of the same colour—sides on foot white nearer to the exterior red lines thickly clouded by 'pale blacking purple'; animals beautifully coloured—foot beneath with white specks—but a few black dots on edge and more on head—length of body one inch, not so narrow in proportion as other species; anterior extremity not nearly so much lengthened—the body in consequence of more uniform breadth. . . . Having found two species is fortunate as it more firmly establishes this new subdivision of the genus *Planaria*.

Notice that Darwin does not try to write in complete sentences. He quickly gets down as many essential details as possible. These details will be an invaluable record later. Writing quickly but accurately, he is able to record information that will be helpful to him in the future.

As you begin to keep a notebook, you will find that it helps you sharpen your eye for observation—a handy talent in anyone training for the technical professions. The habit of attentive observation—and of then recording those observations—is one you'll need not only at school, but at work. Properly kept notebooks become prime evidence if there is litigation or a contest for patent rights. Such litigation occurs throughout the technical professions. Notebooks are primary corroboration should you have to prove origin or substantiate your statements or conclusion.

The case of Alexander Graham Bell is a famous example of a notebook being used to substantiate a claim. Bell filed his patent application for the telephone in 1875, but he was promptly sued by one Daniel Drawbaugh, who claimed that the invention was his own. Drawbaugh produced witnesses at court who testified he had discussed a crude telephone with them. This personal testimony, though, was not enough for the Supreme Court, which rejected Drawbaugh's claims largely on the basis of his inability to produce a single properly dated piece of paper describing the invention.

Gordon Gould provides another famous example. In 1959, he filed an application for a laser patent, but he didn't get it. Instead, in 1960, Charles Townes and his brother-in-law Arthur Schawlow were awarded the basic laser patent.

Gould went to court, claiming he was the inventor of the laser and therefore entitled to the rights. Gould's challenge was based in part on a page from his research notebook. The page had a sketch, a statement of the main idea, and a derivation of the acronym LASER (light amplification by stimulated emission of radiation).

In October 1977, after a series of litigated oppositions, Gould was granted a patent for optically pumped laser amplifiers. The world market has been estimated at between $100 million and $200 million.

So if you think that keeping a notebook is just another chore, think again. It may be one of your best allies in developing your skills in the laboratory, as a writer and perhaps even, as an inventor. Keeping a laboratory notebook will certainly help you write better laboratory reports, both now and in the future.

Finding Time to Write, Often a Section at a Time

At school and at work, few people have long stretches of uninterrupted time. Instead, they have many jobs, writing being just one of them. At work, for example, people are expected to spend the better part of their days doing their technical tasks (for instance, measuring, evaluating, processing, or training) and to squeeze their writing into the occasional free hour. At school, you probably juggle competing demands of classwork, laboratory assignments, responsibilities at home, and perhaps even part-time employment. When your schedule fills in this way, you soon realize that it is rare to have long stretches of time to work uninterruptedly on writing.

That may be part of the reason that staying up all night seems like a promising option, at least the first few times.

Writing takes time if you are going to do a good job. How can you handle this, both at school and later at work? Many people learn to meet the demands of writing with a new strategy—instead of hoping for a long stretch of time, (a hope that rarely materializes), they divide the writing into sections and work on a section at a time, adapting to the shorter uninterrupted periods of time available to them.

You may want to consider this strategy. Because reports lend themselves to a division into introduction, procedure, results, and conclusions, it is fairly easy to work on them a section at a time. You might also want to think about what times of day are more productive for you to tackle a section of your report. Many people work more easily in the morning, others late in the afternoon. Knowing this, they squeeze an hour's writing in the morning, say, when they are better able to tackle the job than, for instance, in the late afternoon when they are fairly fatigued.

You also need to think about how long you can work with high concentration. One hour? Two hours? Many people find they can concentrate for only a few hours on actual writing before their attention wanders.

Guarding against Distraction

You'll have to think hard about your writing habits if you want to shift from a pattern of last-minute writing to one in which you allow time for both writing and revision.

Writing is hard work. When the time comes to write, anything may become a distraction, from reading the dictionary to an urgent conversation on an otherwise routine matter. One of the main things you'll need to do is to identify your favorite distractions—perhaps talking on the telephone, playing with the computer, or visiting with friends. Then you must learn to avoid them—and all other distractions—during the time you've allotted to writing.

Taking Advantage of the Report Format

You may be able to use the fairly fixed format of reports to your advantage as you begin to write.

Reports have standard sections. (See Chapter 1 for a fuller discussion.) Each has long-established functions:

- The abstract gives a synopsis of the findings and their significance.
- The introduction gives the background by defining the problem or issue and its significance; then it provides a brief overview of the report that follows.
- The procedural section tells the method employed in doing the reported work.
- The results section gives a summary of the data, including any statistical manipulation.
- The discussion section interprets and compares results, draws conclusions if there is sufficient evidence, and looks to the future.

Each of these sections has so fixed a function that a good part of report writing is sorting or organizing the information into the appropriate categories. Robert S. Day, author of *How to Write and Publish a Scientific Paper*, puts the matter bluntly: "I take the position that the preparation of a scientific paper has almost nothing to do with literary skill. It is a question of *organization*." What is true for scientific papers is also true for their close relatives, laboratory reports.

Tactics for Turning the Report Format to Your Advantage

As you start to organize your information into the time-honored categories of the report, consider the following tactics:

Making an Outline

Try using the "boilerplate" of report format to help divide the writing into manageable parts. It's a truism that writing is often easier if it's approached in smaller, manageable pieces rather than as one seamless project. Because of the inherent structure of reports, their subdivisions can be the basis for your outline. Try translating the subdivisions into a rough outline, and see if you have five or six manageable parts to think about.

If you have trouble making an outline, consider these standard tactics:

A. Try building an outline using lists.
  1. Jot down each point or idea in a few words.
  2. Make each item short enough to move around.
  3. Jot down examples of points.
  4. Pause. Go back to the list. Draw lines from examples to ideas.
  5. Cross out duplications. Reorder. Group points.
  6. Arrange points so that they follow logically.
  7. Turn the list into a rough outline.

B. Try building an outline by talking to colleagues.
  1. Discuss the points you think you want to make.
  2. Write them down as you talk.
  3. See which ideas are clear to your colleagues and which are not.

4. As you elaborate, jot down the explanations and examples you come up with.

5. Use these explanations and examples as a beginning of your rough outline.

C. Try building an outline by freewriting.

1. Start anywhere, including the middle, and write for 15 minutes.

2. Ignore spelling, grammar, and usage.

3. Try to slide in sentences like "The key point here is that . . ." and "Another key point is that . . ."

4. Try the whole process a second time. Underline the main points or any sentences that look promising. Use them to begin writing the rough outline.

Deciding Where to Begin

Consider which parts of your rough outline seem more accessible and which seem more difficult. If you are very nervous about beginning, give serious thought to doing the easiest part first. Once you've built up a bit of momentum in this way, you may find it easier to continue. In report format, the most manageable part for many writers is the procedure. If you keep notes, you will have recorded what you did. This information can be put on the page and revised. Once the information is written down, you may have the impetus to go to a more difficult section.

In *Alice in Wonderland*, the King of Hearts gives this advice: "Begin at the beginning, and go on till you come to the end: then stop." That is certainly the traditional way to go about writing a report. But beginnings are notoriously difficult; they have a way of expanding to fill all the available time.

Consulting Your Notebook

See what information you have at hand in your laboratory notebook, and consider where it might go. Try taking the information in the notebook and sorting it into the categories you have in your outline. You may find that one section already has quite a bit of information. Consider starting with this section, rather than at the beginning of the report, as you will have a head start on writing this section.

Assimilating the Data

If you are not sure you understand your results, try drawing up tables and graphs. These may help you to assimilate the data. Visualizing your data is an important step in the writing process. The tables and graphs may help you clarify and focus your understanding.

Discuss your results with teammates or colleagues. They may be able to help you see patterns in the data; just talking with them may lead you to an understanding that you did not previously have. Take notes while you are talking or have a teammate take notes in case you can use the discussion as a basis for a rough outline.

Steering Clear of Roadblocks

If the introduction seems difficult to write, try sketching in the problem—a visit to the library will help—but postponing a full statement of the introduction until you've written the discussion section. The introduction marks the path for the reader, answering the questions "What is the problem?" and "Why does this problem matter?" You may find it easier to double back and answer these questions after you've written your discussion section.

Of course, the introduction does come first, and a logically minded person may be bothered by starting in the middle with the procedure, and going on to the results and discussions without ever writing a beginning.

If you find it is essential to write out the problem in full before going forward to the rest of the report, then by all means do so. But if you can't initially frame an introduction that states the problem, try doing an end run by starting with the procedure or by tabulating the data and then writing the discussion.

Remember that the beginning of the report and the beginning of many of its sections are frequently the most difficult to write. Often this is because the beginning is where the writer provides a summary for the reader, telling what is coming and why it matters. But it is hard to summarize the direction of an argument you haven't yet made.

Avoid lingering on overviews, introductions, or summaries when you are first getting started. Instead, try sketching in the top of the report (the introductory paragraphs) if you wish, but don't stop to improve them. These revisions may slow you down, and you may lose the impetus you need to get going with the report.

And the revisions may be in vain. By the time you get to the end of the report, you may have substantially altered what you intended to say, expanding one point, deleting another. Your summary statements will need to reflect all these changes. The summaries you spent hours writing at the beginning may be virtually useless by the time you're done with writing the report.

This happens more often than you might think. Many people work their ideas out on paper. By the time they've finished writing, they have ideas that are different from the ones they had initially. The introductions—the places that give the reader a road map—no longer accurately summarize what is coming. When this happens, the writer has to return to the introduction and completely recast it.

To avoid this problem, if you are uncertain about your introduction, spend less time on it or on any of the overview statements in your report. Once you've written the discussion, you can return to the top of the report and write a road map or summary that will guide your readers along the path of your argument.

Writing the Abstract

If you are having difficulties writing the abstract, postpone writing it until the very end, when you've written the introduction, procedure, and discussion. Then take a key sentence from each section of your report:

- A sentence summing up your objective. If you don't have one, now is the time to include it.
- A sentence summing up your procedure. Remember, though, that in the abstract it's a mistake to dwell on procedural details. Instead, use only enough words to give readers the context. You need to leave room for what matters—your results and conclusions.
- A sentence or two summing up your results.
- A sentence or two summing up your conclusions.
- A sentence summing up the implications or recommendations, if appropriate.

Stitch these sentences together until you have an abstract of the report.

Completing Individual Sections

If you are working a section at a time, concentrate on completing an entire section with the time available, since finishing the section, however roughly, may save trouble tomorrow. If necessary, use very broad strokes to do the job. Omit words; skip what you can fill in later. One scientist commented on his writing, "I always try to go straight through a particular section. If I can't think of a word, I just put in parentheses and go back later to clean it up. Otherwise, I may get bogged down. And if I stop halfway through and then return the next day, I find I have to repeat a lot of the work. I lose the focus of the section."

Making the Most of Initial Drafts

Think about ways to make the most of your first and second drafts. Don't use up your critical faculties by minutely inspecting first drafts of a section for spelling errors. Save that necessary step for later in the writing process. (See Chapters 4 and 5 for details on style, usage, grammar, and punctuation.)

Instead, use that first draft to set forth your major ideas. Ask yourself, Have I covered my major points? Go back to your outline and make sure you have actually developed your major arguments. It is easy to leave essential information out in the pressure of writing.

Many writers work out their ideas on paper—they discover what they are going to say during the actual process of composition. If you compose this way, in the course of writing a first draft

- You may omit the main point of a passage or fail to state it until the end of the passage, in part because you are uncertain of the main point until you've finished composing the passage.
- You may omit transitions or bridges from one section of the report to the next, in part because you are undecided on the direction the argument should take.

- You may either omit essential information or give it in too much detail.
- You may repeat information, particularly if you are interrupted during writing.

These actions are all a normal part of exploratory writing. Once you have put your ideas down in their crude form, however, you will want to revise the text in a second draft so that the report is more readable.

Consider these questions:

- Is the information organized so that readers can follow all the main points?
- Have you introduced main points before details supporting the points?
- Are the details complete and correct?
- Is the information beneath your headings and subheadings consistent with the headings and subheadings? Or do you have "fruit salad"—information mixed into one section (say, the procedure) that properly belongs in another section (say, the results)?

Beginning writers often underestimate the importance of transitions, words like *and, but, thus, first, second,* and *therefore* that are useful as clear, unmistakable signposts of the writer's arguments. When you are in the middle of writing a report, the internal logic of the paper may be obvious to you. However, it may not be as apparent to your readers. For them, transitional words and phrases can function as an outline. Consider ways to use them. Add emphasis with *in fact* or *indeed;* add contrast with *but, although, however, yet,* or *instead;* show addition with *also, in addition,* or *furthermore;* express qualification with *virtually, most,* or *almost* all.

Using a Computer

The computer can help you, but it can also be a terrific time-waster. You may find yourself sitting at the computer wandering the World Wide Web, reading your e-mail, or playing with a sentence that you've written instead of actually writing. Meanwhile, time passes and the basic work of organizing the logic and content of your report remains undone.

Be very aware of the temptations of the computer as you sit down to write. Of course, you can also use the computer as a tool in writing the report more efficiently.

1. Try typing your outline at the beginning of the file. You can call it up when you wander, and use it to help keep on course. Revise the outline as needed as your report develops.

2. Try typing the notes from your laboratory notebook into the appropriate sections of the outline. In this way you will build the sections of the report.

3. Be aware of the limits of revising on the screen rather than on paper. Many people revise directly on the screen. This works to a degree, but may be less effective than you think. That is because organizational errors are hard to spot on the small screen.

For instance, you may have ordered the paragraphs in a section illogically, or left out important information, or been inconsistent in the information you gave in the sections of the report. You may have stated your objective one way in the introduction and another way in the conclusion. This sort of problem is difficult to note when you are looking at a video monitor that shows only a portion of the screen. Instead, print the report and edit from the paper copy. This will provide you with the larger canvas that you need to spot errors that run through the entire report.

Postponing the Final Steps

Consider postponing editing for spelling, grammar, and usage until late in the writing process, however urgent these matters are. Instead, try for content and organization in earlier drafts. Put off decisions on verb tense, point of view, spelling of proper nouns, and the dozens of other important aspects of style and grammar until later, if you are able. Instead, think about using the time you've set aside to concentrate on what you have to say (the content) and on ways to organize this content. Content and organization are big mountains to climb. In some ways, it may be easier to work on the wording of sentences than it is to shape the entire document. If so, do the shaping first and fine-tune the wording afterwards.

Letting the Report Sit

Let the report rest for a few hours before you revise it. Problems with logic and organization are hard to spot when you have just written portions of the report and are rereading them. If you leave the sections of the report for a few hours or even overnight, you can return to them with a better chance of having the outside eyes of a critic. Lapses in the organization will be easier to see and to correct.

Editing for Style and Usage

4

Outline

Changing from Writer to Editor

Chapters 1 through 3 discussed your role as a *writer* of laboratory reports:

- Chapter 1 and Chapter 2 gave the parts of the report and the type of information in each part. This is formal information best read *before* you write.
- Chapter 3 discussed strategies for transforming the raw materials of an experiment into a report. This is process information best read *while* you are drafting your report.

Those three chapters should help you get the content of your report down on paper in an organized way.

But once you've articulated all of your main points and organized them within report format, one final step remains—editing your work for style, grammar, usage, and punctuation.

When you switch from being the *writer* of the report to the *editor*, you'll change your focus from *composing* (actually shaping your thoughts) to *editing* what you've written (making important changes in the wording of the report).

Of course, you probably thought about the wording of your sentences as you were composing the report, but to fine-tune your wording effectively, you'll find it useful to dedicate an hour or two after you've finished the rough draft solely to this editing task.

Editing is the subject of Chapters 4 and 5. When you are the editor, you return to the report with the perspective of an outsider, casting a cold eye on the text, and then selecting, trimming, and focusing the language so that your message is as clear as possible.

In the matter of style, Chapter 4 addresses these issues:

- Insertion of definitions, abbreviations, and acronyms into the narrative.
- Governing verb tense in each section of the report.
- Use of *I* and *we* (first-person pronouns) in the narrative.
- Use of *he* as the governing third-person singular.
- Representation of numbers in figures or words.
- Consistency and precision of language in technical text.

In the matter of usage, Chapter 4 discusses the small choices in language that writers make (for instance, between *affect* and *effect* or between *imply* and *infer*), the treatment of Greek and Latin terminology in science, and other confusibles like *adverse* versus *averse* and *expect* versus *anticipate*.

Matters of Style   Definitions, Abbreviations, and Acronyms

When should you stop to define a term you are using?

- When you think the term may be unfamiliar to the reader.

- When you think the reader may know the general use of the term, but not the narrow or specific way in which you are using it.
- When the term is easily confused with another term.
- When the term is a governing one (that is, when it's crucial to the underlying argument that you are making).

Whether you insert definitions in your text depends on the background of your readers—on how much they know before you begin, and how much more you decide to tell them.

If you are an electrical engineer writing for other electrical engineers, you are safe using the abbreviations of your field—other EEs will know what an IC is. (But if you are not an electrical engineer, you may wonder whether IC means, for instance, integrated circuit or ion chromatography.)

Often you will be writing your report not just for people in your field, but for people with a variety of technical backgrounds. If so, you'll need to write out unfamiliar terms in full on first use and then follow with an abbreviated form and a definition.

Sometimes the definition is just a synonym or short explanatory phrase enclosed in parentheses. For instance, in one report in Chapter 2, the author defines surfactant this way:

> [I]t is possible to determine if the molecules are surfactants (molecules localized to the particle surface).

Sometimes the definition of a term will include etymological information (information related to the origin of the word).

> The modem (for modulator-demodulator) is a device that can be attached to convert the computer's digital signals into signals for transmission over telephone lines.

> Bits (short for binary digits) are units describing the information contents of any message.

If you are using an abbreviation or acronym, it should follow the first use of the term and be enclosed in parentheses.

> In its current form as an aerosol particle fluorescence microscope (APFM), the microscope is affixed with optical filters and polarizers for recording images in inelastic fluorescence scattering.

Abbreviations (for example, IC) are pronounced as letters; acronyms (for example, LASER) are pronounced as words. On first reference, use full spelling of the term followed by the shortened form in parentheses. For subsequent references, use the shortened form.

At one time, periods or points were used after each letter in abbreviations or acronyms but today more and more style sheets permit you to represent abbreviations without periods.

Most abbreviations, including abbreviations for units of measure like *amp*, *Hz*, *cal*, *cm*, *hr*, *hp*, *sec*, and *rad*, no longer use points.

One exception to this is abbreviations that might be misread as words. Thus, the abbreviations for the units of measure *at.*, *gal.*, and *no.* have points, as otherwise they might be construed as the words *at*, *gal*, and *no*.

Note that if the abbreviation falls at the end of a sentence, one period is enough. Do not add a second one.

Example 1 An introduction with undefined terms

In the past year only a trickle of money on the World Wide Web has actually made its way toward consumer goods such as books, flowers, and airline tickets. But the Web has actually produced a bona fide financial hit—intranets.

[What are intranets?]
[What are extranets?]

Intranets (and extranets) are the emerging bourgeoisie of the Internet—stable, productive money earners that are becoming the economic bedrock of cyberspace.

Example 2 An introduction with new terms defined

In the past year only a trickle of money on the World Wide Web has actually made its way toward consumer goods such as books, flowers, and airline tickets. But the Web has actually produced a bona fide financial hit—intranets. Intranets are networks that are generally accessible only to select users and that rely on the rules of the Internet that permit computers to "talk" to one another.

[The author decides to define intranets, a relatively new term for readers, but not World Wide Web, as the term is very familiar to readers.]

Intranets (and extranets, or networks extended to branches and business partners) are the emerging bourgeoisie of the Internet—stable, productive money earners that are becoming the economic bedrock of cyberspace.

[The author inserts a definition of extranets, a new term, but does not define the extremely familiar cyberspace.]

In your English classes, you have probably been taught to "stay in the same tense."

This is good advice. However, in technical and scientific reports, this good advice has a special twist, for the rules for tense are slightly different in science than in English classes.

The difference is that the governing tense—the main tense in which you tell the story—may change from section to section of a report. That means that even though the report is a whole, in the same way that an essay is a complete document, the tense in which you tell the report is not continuous—it varies according to what you are saying within the report.

The governing tense of the introduction is the present tense. In this section you are telling the reader what the problem or issue is that you are addressing. You may also use the present perfect tense if your work started in the past and extends into the present.

Here is the introduction from the example used in Chapter 2, slightly shortened, with the verbs italicized.

Introduction

Microparticles in air, such as biological spores or other aerosol particles, *partake* in biological reproduction and in the dissemination of disease [1]; *provide* small "test tubes" for brewing acid rain; and *are* a subject of continual environmental monitoring. [2] Although such particles *are* commonly investigated by collecting the particles on filter paper for spectrochemical analyses, this method *can* corrupt the particles in several ways. Contact *can* easily lead to chemical contamination, physical distortion, and charge transfer.

We have *introduced* a means for investigating a single aerosol particle "in situ," through microphotography on a levitated particle. [4] In addition to contributing to the construction and design of the microscope, our work *has expanded* into fluorescence microphotography. By spectrally resolving microphotographs of levitated microdroplets containing fluorescent molecules, it *is* possible to determine if the molecules *are* surfactants (molecules localized to the particle surface).

In what follows we describe our aerosol particle fluorescence microscope (APFM), *discuss* the preparation of individual particles, *present* results on the fluorescence microphotography of surfactant chromophores, and *discuss* these results in terms of the physics of fluorescence and the physical chemistry of molecules at a liquid's surface.

While the governing tense of the introduction is the present, the governing tense of the procedure is the past, for in this section you are telling what you *did* during the experiment. Use the simple past tense unless you are describing an action that happened before another action in the past. In this case, use the past perfect. (We *examined* the oscilloscope after it *had been subjected* to a severe shock.)

Here is a selection from an example used in Chapter 2, slightly shortened, with the verbs italicized:

Experimental Work

In the first part of the experiment, a function generator *was connected* directly to the oscilloscope to obtain an image on the scope. Afterwards, the point-to-point voltage of the image *was measured and converted* to RMS voltage.

In the experiment, the voltage on the function generator *was set* to 2 V RMS, and then the DMM *was used* to determine the voltage output of the generator more accurately. After the signal *was measured* with the DMM, it *was confirmed* with the oscilloscope, which measured the peak-to-peak voltage from the image of the sine wave on the oscilloscope screen.

The second part of the experiment *tested* the accuracy of the frequency of the sine waves generated by the signal generator. To do this, the trigger *was set* to Line, which is 60 Hz. The frequency of the function generator was then *changed* to observe the settings for which one could observe a stationary image. Afterwards, a short table comparing actual frequencies with the dial setting on the generator *was prepared*.

In the third part of the experiment, the advantages and disadvantages of the two modes of operating the oscilloscope *were compared:* dc and ac coupling modes. Once a sine wave *was displayed* on the oscilloscope, the dc offset of the function generator *was varied.* That *added* a constant voltage to the sine wave. The change in the image using dc vs. ac coupling modes *was* then *observed.* A square wave *was* then *substituted* for a sine wave, and the comparison of dc and ac *made* again.

The governing tense of the discussion is the present, for in this section you are arguing for what you think is so.

Since the transition moment of ORDB *is known* to lie in the plane of the three aromatic rings, our measurement for the direction of the transition moment *is consistent* with the plane of the rings being parallel with the plane of the particle's surface.

The results *show* that it *is* possible to estimate the orientation of a surfactant molecule on a liquid's surface through long-term fluorescent imaging of doped aerosol particles.

The author of the report quoted above and in Chapter 2 also used the *past tense* in the discussion when he spoke of actions in the past, and the *future tense* to suggest applications of the research.

First-Person Pronouns

Can you use the pronouns *we* and *I* in the reports that you write? Is it correct to say, "I observed" or "we observed," or must you say "It was observed that" to avoid using *I* or *we*?

Whether to use first-person pronouns *(I, we)* or a passive cliche like "it was observed that" has been a controversial issue in technical and scientific writing since the turn of the century.

It may surprise you to learn that at one time all scientists used *we* and *I*. In fact, from the Renaissance to the early twentieth century, *we* and *I* were entirely acceptable words in scientific discourse. In 1615, for instance, Harvey wrote in *An Anatomical Disquisition on the Motion of the Heart-Blood in Animals.*

I finally saw that the blood, forced by the action of the left ventricle into the arteries, was distributed to the body at large and its several parts, in the same manner as it is sent through the lungs, impelled by the right ventricle into the right pulmonary artery, and that it then passed through the veins and along the vena cava, and so round to the left ventricle in the manner already indicated, which motion we may be allowed to call circular.

In 1869, first person was still alive and well when Joseph Lister reported to the British Medical Association that "In the course of an extended investigation into the nature of inflammation, and the healthy and morbid conditions of the blood in relation to it, I arrived, several years ago, at the conclusion that the essential cause of suppuration in wounds is decomposition."

But in the early twentieth century, the first person fell out of favor among those who decided they would sound "more objective" if they did not include references to themselves. To do this, they removed the first person, and substituted for it what is called in grammar *passive voice*—that is, they substituted "it was observed" for "I saw," and "it was demonstrated that" for "we demonstrated."

What is the difference between active and passive voices? The active voice emphasizes the subject of the sentence:

Smith examined the spectra.

The passive voice emphasizes the object:

The spectra were examined.

The passive is formed by a combination of the verb *to be* and the past participle *(were + examined)*. It may contain a "by" clause if the writer wishes *(by Smith)*.

The spectra were examined by Smith.

In the 1980s, a second trend reinforced the use of passive voice in science and technology. U.S. companies developed a strong belief in the importance of teamwork, and when they did, the use of *I* fell completely out of favor. It was considered an egocentric, highly inappropriate pronoun for team-driven efforts. *We*, however, was acceptable.

Today it is possible to use *we* if you work for a company, but less possible to use *I* because of its historical associations.

Scientific journals are fighting for the use of *I* and *we*—or at least *we*—urging their readers to use the first person when appropriate, particularly in the introduction and conclusion to a paper, where the author's voice is most clearly heard discussing and interpreting.

However, *I* remains suspect, so most people working in science and technology find themselves opting for the old-fashioned, very useful passive voice when the choice lies between the passive and the forbidden *I*.

As a rule of thumb, use the passive when the performer is irrelevant to, or less important than, the object; avoid it when the focus belongs on the subject. Thus, use "The engineering staff assessed the damage" to accent the staff, but "Damages were assessed" if you don't know who did the assessing, if you don't care who did the assessing, if who did the assessing doesn't matter, or if the damage is the most important element in the sentence.

When you do use passive voice, you'll probably have to disregard the disconcerting warnings from the grammar checker on your word processor; most grammar programs include alerts on overuse of the passive voice.

He as the Governing Third-Person Singular

While English offers a third-person plural pronoun that includes both masculine and feminine *(they, them)*, it lacks such a pronoun for third-person singular *(he, she, him, her)*. This leads to a problem when the writer uses a term like *everyone, everybody, each person,* or *one,* for these words all require a singular pronoun. The historical solution has been to use a masculine pronoun:

> Each person in the lab should maintain his notebook carefully.

This sort of sentence, though, excludes females. One solution to this exclusionary language is to change singular antecedents to plurals:

> Students should maintain their notebooks carefully.

Another solution is to recast the sentence:

> Notebooks should be maintained carefully.

Some writers use *he or she,* although others find the phrase cumbersome.

Representing Numbers—Figures versus Words

When should you write out numbers as words, and when may you simply represent them in figures? This is a confusing issue, for numbers are written out far more often in literary writing than in technical fields. Still, there are some occasions in technical text when numbers should be represented as words rather than figures. Here are guidelines:

1. Use figures
   with units of measure:

0.40 mg, 4 sec

   in a mathematical or chemical context:

5 orders of magnitude, a factor of 8

for items and sections:

Sample 1, Unit 3

for figures and tables:

Figure 1, Table 1

for all numbers in a series, even if a particular item in the series might ordinarily be spelled out:

Panels 1, 2, and 3 included 2, 4, and 8 subjects, respectively.

2. Use words
for numbers below 10, both cardinal and ordinal, unaccompanied by a unit of measure:

three pipettes but 30 pipettes

fifth trial but 30th trial

for numbers below 10, even when accompanied by a unit of measure, if the use is not technical:

Last year I worked on the project for two months.

for numbers that begin sentences:

Twenty-one students participated in the project.

(You can also, of course, recast the sentence to avoid spelling out *twenty-one:* Participating in the project were 21 students.)

for common fractions:

One-fourth of the sample

If you use two consecutive numerical expressions, either spell out one expression or recast the sentence:

Fourteen 5-part packets accompanied the set.
(not 14 5-part packets).

These rules also apply to adjectival forms:

A five-year-old sample

A 30-hour trial

Consistency and Precision in Technical Language

Whether you are speaking or writing, certain constraints in the rhetoric of scientific and technical writing will influence how you present your ideas.

Literary writing is the search to create what poet Marianne Moore calls "imaginary gardens with real toads in them"—to present a flashing, psychologically correct setting in which readers suddenly come upon their own experiences with the shock of recognition.

Scientific writing does not speak in this tongue. Instead, one finds an avoidance of impressionistic detail, of language that is obviously emotive or suggestive. In other words, the writer struggles to reduce the emotional involvement of the reader's response rather than to evoke it.

Elaborate prose is rare. The author attempts to transmit information as objectively as possible, with language the admitted enemy in this endeavor. Language can be rife with ambiguity; emotional associations cluster around words. It is the technical professional's job to cut away at this ambiguity. Precision and consistency are hallmarks of the style.

As an aid, scientists often invent words that are not in everyday use and therefore not likely to evoke irrelevant associations in the reader's mind. For example, when Faraday finished his work on electrolysis, he visited William Whewell (at that time a professor of moral philosophy at Cambridge University in England) to have an untarnished set of words coined for his results. That is how the terms *anode* and *cathode* came into existence.

The people who coin technical and scientific terms specifically to limit their connotations often watch, aghast, as the public embraces these words and in so doing corrupts their meanings.

The broadening in popular use of the term *quantum* (plural, *quanta*) is a good example of this process. Used by Planck, Einstein, and Bohr, the term had a distinct meaning. It referred to small, discrete amounts of energy. The term, when adopted by the public, soon became *quantum leap*, meaning a large amount. A television show used the expression to refer to the weekly leaps of a hero trapped in a time machine. While the term bears some vestiges of its original definition, the precision of its meaning is gone.

The rigor and consistency of scientific and technical vocabulary distinguish it from the vocabulary of more general writing. For example, in many types of literary writing, students are taught to avoid repeating words and instead to find synonyms. In technical and scientific writing, consistency—rather than switching from one term to a possible synonym—is highly valued, whether in a report for the Food and Drug Administration or instructions for using a machine. Changing terminology can confuse the reader of the document.

Color in technical and scientific writing is rare, and for good reason. Consider, for instance, this letter that Charles Babbage (inventor of the precursor to the modern computer) wrote to Tennyson, the English poet:

Sir,

In your otherwise beautiful poem there is a verse which reads

Every moment dies a man,
Every moment one is born.

It must be manifest that if this were true, the population of the world would be at a standstill. In truth the rate of birth is slightly in excess of that of death. I would suggest that in the next edition of your poem you have it read

> *Every moment dies a man,*
> *Every moment 1 1/16 is born.*

Strictly speaking this is not correct, the actual figure is so long that I cannot give it into a line, but I believe the figure 1 1/16 will be sufficiently accurate for poetry.

Babbage takes issue with the poet Tennyson for figurative use of the expression, "every moment dies a man." The accuracy of language in poetry is very different from the accuracy of language in scientific and technical literature. True, it is possible to find an occasional figure of speech in technical text. For instance, R. W. Wood describes spectra as "furrowed," and Woodward in the *Journal of the American Chemical Society* once described the strychnine molecule as a "tangled skein of atoms." In general, though, the language of science and technology is remarkably austere. Figurative language is infrequent. Narrative voice is scant. And humor is very rare. Usually, the speaker is shoved firmly into the background, and organization and logic become the mainstays of explication.

The one form of figurative language used by both poets and technical writers is comparison, although often it's used in its plainest forms rather than in metaphors or analogies.

Thomas Edison wrote in his notebook, "I am experimenting upon an instrument which does for the Eye what the phonograph does for the Ear, which is the recording and reproduction of things in motion."

Comparison is often used to bring numbers to life on a page. Here is Richard Feynmann, explaining tests of the theory of quantum electrodynamics:

> I'll give you some recent numbers: experiments have Dirac's number at 1.00115965221 (with an uncertainty of about 4 in the last digit); the theory puts it at 1.00115965246 (with an uncertainty of about five times as much). To give you a feeling for the accuracy of these numbers, it comes out something like this: If you were to measure the distance from Los Angeles to New York for this accuracy, it would be exact to the thickness of a human hair. That's how delicately quantum electrodynamics has, in the past fifty years, been checked—both theoretically and experimentally.

There are some cases, though, where comparison is not the right technique. "Make measurements in centimeters, not in fruits, vegetables, or nuts," a medical textbook advises. "Pea-sized, lemon-sized and walnut-sized lesions vaguely convey an idea, but make accurate evaluations and future comparisons impossible. How big were the lemons or peas? Does the walnut have a shell?" Walnuts come in different sizes; the comparison is not useful for the audience that needs not a flash of insight, but specific dimensions.

Matters of Usage

When you are involved in writing a report and therefore very busy struggling with the content, the finer points of language like usage are best put aside. But later, when you revise your document, you'll want to think about how you use each word within a sentence.

Correct usage plays an important part in clear language. Readers respond to the small, careful choices in language good writers make. Did you say "affect" when you meant "effect"? Of such small distinctions as those between *affect* and *effect* is language made.

Questions of usage perplex students, in part because guidelines for what does and does not constitute correct usage (linguistic propriety) change fairly quickly in the United States, where no official group or academy opposes the introduction of, say, the expression "Author the report" to mean "Write the report."

English adapts to change—in fact, some linguists speculate that this openness to the new or the adapted—such as from *floppy disc* to *software* to *menu*—is one of the reasons English has become the international language of science.

Such rapid change means that some usages we were taught were unacceptable at age 12 may be perfectly proper within five or six years. In the 1950s, for example, usage handbooks advised students to use *contact* only as a noun, never as a verb.

Some changes, like using *contact* as a verb, are settled by gradual academic capitulation to popular speech. Today, *contact* is a perfectly acceptable verb—you can *contact* your instructor by e-mail whenever you wish—but the jury is still out on *aliquotting* your samples or *portholing* your data.

Many changes that are popular in speech have only marginal acceptance in formal discourse. Thus we have a new group of people who intend to *author* their reports, although traditionalists still prefer to *write* them.

Some usage changes are inevitable. Arguing against them, as the linguist Geoffry Nunberg once commented, is like a landscape gardener arguing with continental drift.

Other changes, though, are fended off by spirited argument. *Irregardless* is still rejected as a proper word by many dictionaries at this writing, although it will probably gain currency in the future. (It is already in *Webster's*.) Using *data* as a singular was disputed hotly as early as 1900; the use of "the data is" remains controversial even today. While most academics still construe the term as a plural ("these data are . . ."), many popular writers now routinely use "data" as a collective singular.

Sometimes the fight is over loss of a distinction (as in the confusion of *imply* and *infer*, or *respectively* and *each*); other issues are strictly grammatical, as in using *impact* as a verb.

Should we worry about when and why to prefer *fewer* to *lesser*, or *dilemma* to *problem?*

Some people dismiss usage distinctions as linguistic niceties of little or no concern to technical writing. Others vigorously uphold usage distinctions that are gradually being erased by popular speech (*disinterested* versus *uninterested; accurate* versus *precise*).

Here are some standard usage issues at the time of this writing that may help you in editing the wording of your reports.

Adapt, adopt

Adapt means "to adjust or modify":

We *adapted* the software so it would run on a Macintosh.

Adopt means "to take up, accept, or choose":

The Freshman Engineering Committee *adopted* a new textbook.

Adverse, averse

Averse means "unwilling":

The group was *averse* to a change in the procedure.

Adverse means "unfavorable":

We hope the change will have no *adverse* effects.

Affect, effect

Effect is the noun in this pair of confusible words. As a noun, it is always marked by *a, an,* or *the:*

The *effect* of cold temperatures on some of the lab equipment is quite marked.

Affect is a verb meaning "to act upon or influence":

Cold temperatures *affect* some of the equipment in the lab.

(*Effect* may also be a verb, meaning "to carry out" or "accomplish" in such bureaucratic expressions as "We *effected* a change in the laboratory.")

Allot, a lot

To allot is to apportion:

We *allotted* equal shares to each person.

A lot is a great deal. Note that *a lot* comprises two words, not one:

We had *a lot* more material than we needed.

All together, altogether

Altogether means "completely":

> There are *altogether* too many requirements for this class.

All together means "in a group":

> Usually we work in teams. We are *all together* only for lectures.

Alternate, alternative

Alternative applies to two or more choices:

> We can choose Method A or, *alternatively*, we can choose Method B.

Alternate applies to something that happens in successive turns:

> *Alternating* current.

Amount, number

Use *number*, not *amount*, for countable units:

> The *number* of computer science majors increases each year.

not

> The amount of computer science majors increases each year.

Anticipate, expect

To *anticipate* is to prepare for:

> Because we *anticipated* difficulties in this part of the experiment, we prepared carefully.

Expect does not imply any preparation.

Compound words and modifiers

Compound words, formed by the combination of two words or more, are an important source of new vocabulary in technical English.

One aspect of compound words that may confuse you is the variety of ways they can be spelled. When new compounds first gain currency, they may be spelled as a solid *(workstation)*. But they may also appear in an open form *(work station)*. They may even appear hyphenated *(work-station)*.

All three forms are usually correct initially—it takes a while for a new coinage to acquire a standard form. As new words begin to establish themselves in the language, they are as likely to appear open *(word processor)* as solid *(online)*; hyphens tend to disappear. In general, the progression in U.S. English is from open to solid as a compound becomes established as a permanent vocabulary item.

The latest usage for established compounds will be in your dictionary, provided it is current. For very recent coinages, you'll have to check with your professional society (for instance, the Institute for Electronic and Electrical Engineers or the American Chemical Society) to find out the preferred way to represent new compounds.

Data

Today the word *data*, which is the plural of the Latin *datum*, is increasingly construed as a singular (There is not enough *data* to draw a conclusion.). However, the plural form is firmly established for more formal uses (These *data* suggest that . . .).

If you are speaking of one fact or datum, try "one item of data." See also "Greek and Latin words and expressions," below.

e.g., i.e.

The common error is to mistake *e.g.* (an abbreviation for *exempli gratia*, "for example" in Latin) for *i.e.* (an abbreviation for *id est*, "that is to say" in Latin).

Eponyms

Eponyms (names based on persons or places) are frequently used in science and technology to describe an instrument *(Bunsen burner)*, a field of study *(Raman spectroscopy)*, a phenomenon *(the Einstein-Podolsky-Rosen paradox)* or a test method or procedure *(the Stockbarger method)*.

Capitalize the eponym, not the modifiers:

Planck constant
Oppenheimer approximation

Fewer, less than

The traditional distinction is to use *fewer* for that which is individual and countable:

Do not use this equipment if you have *fewer* than 10 samples.

Use *less than* for amounts:

We have *less* fuel on hand *than* we expected.

Greek and Latin words and expressions

The trend in Greek and Latin words is to prefer the English or anglicized version. Thus *appendixes* are replacing *appendices* in many reports, and *formulas* are overtaking *formulae*.

Still, many Greek and Latin plurals remain, among them *criteria, spectra, phenomena, crises, bases, axes, hypotheses, media, strata,* and *data*. If you preserve the language of the original plural *(phenomena, criteria, data)*, remember that any modifiers must be plural too. Do not use "One criteria is" or "One phenomena is."

Principal, principle

A principle is a guiding rule:

> *Principles of Scientific Investigation* is by E. Bright Wilson.

Principal is an adjective meaning "first in importance":

> The *principal* problem with this program is its complexity.

Principal as a noun refers to a head or central performer:

> She is the *principal* in the investigation.

Respectively

Respectively means "in the order given," not "each" or "one by one." Therefore in this sentence, *respectively* is misused:

> The two lasers have wavelengths of 488 nm and 467 nm, *respectively*.

Instead, use *respectively* to link two or more groups within a sentence:

> The argon laser and the xenon laser have wavelengths of 488 nm and 467 nm, *respectively*.

Respectively is considered to be parenthetic, so it's set off by commas.

Editing for Grammar and Punctuation

5

Outline

Close Editing Close editing for grammar and punctuation is often done late in the writing process rather than at the beginning, when writers have to maintain their impetus by getting ideas down and organizing them coherently.

Chapter 5 presents basic troublespots in grammar and punctuation that you are likely to confront as you edit your reports.

In matters of *grammar*, the classic pitfalls for students proofreading their reports often involve

- Agreement in number of subject and verb.
- Errors in parallel structure.
- Misplaced or dangling modifiers.
- Use of collective nouns.
- Use of pronouns.

Punctuation problems in reports usually concern the use of the apostrophe, the colon, the comma, ellipses, hyphens, parentheses and brackets, and semicolons.

Some errors, such as misplaced modifiers, are the same as those examined in English class; others, like rapid changes in hyphenation for technical terms, are different.

Here are some guidelines for each of these areas.

Matters of Grammar ## Agreement in Number of Subject and Verb

This sentence has a grammatical error:

> The microscope and associated apparatus consists of an electrodynamic levitator trap equipped with lateral-centering electrodes, a homemade microscope, and a cooled integrating CCD camera.

The error is in the verb *consists*. It should be *consist*. Why? Because the subject of the sentence, "microscope and associated apparatus," has two parts, making it a plural subject. (The technical name for subjects joined by *and* is *compound subject*.)

Plural subjects require plural verbs, as singular subjects require singular verbs. Another way to say this is that verb and subject have to agree in number.

Errors in subject–verb agreement are common in reports. Why does this happen? Sometimes the problem lies in sentences so long that the subject is no longer in shouting distance of the verb. Sometimes, though, the error has to do with the writer's ignorance of the many tricky conventions that govern subject–verb agreement. Here is a brief review:

1. Compound subjects (subjects joined by *and*) are usually plural. Not

The compilation of technical information for the report and its use
with graphics and tabular material *is* very important.

But

The *compilation* of technical information for the report *and* its *use*
with graphics and tabular material *are* very important.

The exception is when the compound subject is thought of as one
unit:

Research and development *is* in this wing of the building.

If the compound subject is modified by *each* or *every,* the verb is
singular:

Each computer and printer *is* available.

2. *Each, either, neither, one, anybody,* and *somebody* are always
singular when they are pronoun subjects:

Neither of the instruments *works* well.

3. Ignore objects of prepositions and compound prepositions such
as *along with, in addition to, together with,* and *accompanied by*
when determining the number of the verb:

The *head* of the team, as well as all the other members, *is*
responsible for writing a report.

As can be seen from the table, *substitution* of the benzene ring
with electron donating groups, as well as some electron
withdrawing groups, generally *has* no effects on final product
purity.

4. Collective nouns are usually construed as singular:

The engineering staff *has* voted on the matter.

Collective nouns may be construed as plural, though, if each
member of the group is acting individually:

A number of engineering majors *are* choosing electrical
engineering as a major.

But

The number of engineering majors *is* increasing.

Note that units of measure are usually regarded as collective singulars and therefore take singular verbs:

30 ml *was* added (not *were* added).

5. In *either—or* and *neither—nor* constructions, use a singular verb
when both subjects are singular. If both are plural, use a plural verb.
If one is singular and the other plural, the verb agrees with the nearer
subject:

Neither the device nor the chemicals *have* arrived.
Neither the chemicals nor the device *has* arrived.

6. Noun clauses that are the subject of the sentence take a singular verb:

What this report needs *is* more proofreading.

7. Linking verbs *(am, is, are, was, were, seems, appears)* take their number from the subject (the words before the linking verb), not the complement (the words after the linking verb):

Repeated absences *were* the reason he failed.
The reason he failed *was* repeated absences.
The rigorous calculations *are* the only difficulty with the method.
The only difficulty with the method *is* the rigorous calculations.

Errors in Parallel Construction

In parallel construction all the items joined in a series or comparison have the same grammatical form. For instance, in the sentence, "He often navigates files by moving to the beginning of the line and search for text," the words *moving* and *search* are not parallel. One is an -ing form and the other is an infinitive.

To correct the sentence, try "He often navigates files by *moving* to the beginning of the line and *searching* for text."

In parallel form, adjectives are linked with adjectives, prepositional phrases with prepositional phrases, infinitives with infinitives. In a list, too, all items should be parallel.
Not

Jones made two recommendations:
1. The installation of new mounting blocks to reposition the valves.
2. Add a pneumatic control loop.

But either

Jones made two recommendations:
1. The installation of new mounting blocks to reposition the valves.
2. The addition of a pneumatic control loop.

Or

Jones made two recommendations:
1. Install a new mounting block to reposition the valves.
2. Add a pneumatic control loop.

Here is an error in parallel elements taken from a procedure:

Procedure:
1. Check with safety coordinator to confirm all waste was transferred and accounted for before any burning takes place.

2. Check to see if ash and water effluent-drums are staged.

3. The induction fan on the caustic water system is operational.

The first two items are commands, but the third item is a regular sentence. Therefore, item 3 is not parallel with items 1 and 2. Corrected, the sequence might read

Procedure:

1. Check with safety coordinator to confirm all waste was transferred and accounted for before any burning takes place.

2. Check to see if ash and water effluent-drums are staged.

3. Make sure the induction fan on the caustic water system is operational.

Misplaced or Dangling Modifiers

Readers expect introductory phrases to modify (explain) the subject of the main sentence. Introductory phrases that fail to do this are said to dangle.

For instance, this sentence has a classic misplaced or dangling modifier:

Once captured and balanced in the electrodynamic trap, we irradiated the particle from below with a circular polarized beam from an Argon ion laser.

In the sentence, it sounds as though the authors ("we"), rather than the particle, were captured and balanced in the electrodynamic trap.

This error occurs became the words "once captured and balanced in the electrodynamic trap" are in the wrong place—next to "we" rather than next to the words they modify, "particle." To fix the sentence, place "particle" next to the phrase modifying it:

Once captured and balanced in the electrodynamic trap, the particle is irradiated from below with a circular polarized beam from an Argon ion laser.

Some sentences are best corrected by adding a logical subject. Not

To alter screen position, the blue key must be depressed.

But

To alter screen position, *you* must depress the blue key.

Not

If thought about a while, most people might agree with that statement.

But

If *they* thought for a while, most people might agree with the statement.

Some sentences must be recast to avoid ambiguous modification. In a sentence like "At the meeting, our team joined the mostly French chemists," the meaning of "mostly" is unclear. Try "At the meeting, our team joined the chemists, many of whom were French."

Use of Pronouns

Pronouns must have a noun or pronoun that the reader is sure is the antecedent (the word the pronoun stands for). If the reader must pause to decide on the probable antecedent, you need to recast the sentence to prevent any momentary jolt, ambiguity, or misunderstanding.
Not

> After the *Challenger* accident, NASA engineers, acting on the prodding of an investigatory committee, presented a series of design changes for the O-rings, *which* pleased the committee.

The antecedent of "which" could be "design changes for the O-rings" or the fact that the engineers responded to prodding. To make the sentence clearer, you might change the "which," depending on meaning, as follows:

> After the *Challenger* accident, NASA engineers, acting on the prodding of an investigatory committee, presented a series of design changes for the O-rings, *changes that* pleased the committee.

Pronouns should agree in number with the words they replace: singular antecedent, singular pronoun; plural antecedent, plural pronoun. Therefore, this sentence has an error:

> *Each* person in the group should submit *their* report.

Each, the antecedent, is singular, but *their*, the pronoun, is plural. The pronoun does not agree with its antecedent.
To correct the sentence, try

> Each person in the group should submit a report.

Note that the indefinite pronouns *each, either, everyone, everybody, anybody, anyone, either, neither, one, no one, someone,* and *somebody* are construed as singular:

> Neither of them *is* correct.

Several, both, few, and *many* are construed as plurals:

> Several of the instruments *have* arrived.

All, any, some, most, and *none* are singular or plural depending on meaning or referent. (Look at the prepositional phrase that follows *all, any, some,* or *most.* If its object is plural, use a plural verb.)

All of the *reports have* been submitted.

All of the *substance remains* in the container.

Punctuation of pronominal possessives *(yours, its, his, hers, ours, theirs)* poses other problems. The common error is to confuse *its,* a pronominal possessive that does not take an apostrophe, with *it's,* the contraction of *it* plus *is.*

Not

Its standard procedure to stack the boxes that way.

But

It's standard procedure to stack the boxes that way.

Not

It's cost is high.

But

Its cost is high.

Note that pronominal possessives do not take *'s.*

Not

The report is *her's.*

But

The report is *hers.*

Use of Collective Nouns

In daily conversation outside the laboratory, you may have heard confusing sentences like this:

The couple *is* married.

The couple *are* divorced.

Which is correct? Is the couple a singular ("is") or a plural ("are")?

Actually, both sentences are correct. The verb depends on whether the couple is acting together as a collective singular. Once divorced, they are no longer a collective singular.

Collective nouns are very common in technical writing. For instance, *series*, *variety*, and *combination* are collective nouns used frequently in technical and scientific texts. So long as you view the members of the group as a unit (a collective singular), use singular verbs and pronouns to refer to the group:

> The series *demonstrates* important features of spectroscopic perturbation.

But when you are dealing with individual items use plural verbs and plural pronouns:

> The series of spectra *were transferred* onto transparencies using a laser printer.

Units of measure are collective singulars, and therefore take singular verbs:

> Six quarts *was* added.

In general, plurals of quantity and extent take a singular verb so long as they are viewed as a unit:

> Thirty percent *is* a good response rate.
> Fourteen dollars *is* the unit price.

**Some Useful
Punctuation**

Apostrophes

Use the apostrophe to show possession *(Feynmann's lectures)*, to indicate a contraction *(won't)*, and to form plurals of letters, symbols, and words referred to as words:

> Repetition of q's and r's was common.

In general, you needn't use an apostrophe in all-capitalized abbreviations or acronyms, or for numbers:

> ICs, during the 1990s

Use an apostrophe and *s* to form the possessive singular, including for most nouns ending in *s (Sweiss's notebook)*, but note some famous historical exceptions:

> Gauss' law, Bayes' theorem, Stokes' law

Use an apostrophe to form the possessive of plural nouns ending in *s* or *es:*

> the teams' reports

For all other nouns, add *'s*:

Freshmen's choice

For more than one owner, add the apostrophe to the last name:

Pauling and Wilson's book on quantum mechanics

Pronominal possessives use no apostrophe:

his, hers, its, ours, theirs, yours

Note the apostrophe in expressions such as a *month's delay*.

Colons

Use a colon

1. To introduce a list:

The rank order of activity from the most to the least active agent was as follows: ceftizoxime, ceftriaxone, norfloxacin, and imipenem.

2. To introduce a restatement or explanation. You will hear the words *namely* or *as follows*. If you wish, you may capitalize the initial letter of the restatement or explanation:

Thomas Edison had an inviolate procedure in keeping his laboratory notebooks: He made sure all entries were signed, dated, and properly witnessed.

Commas

Use a comma

1. To set off introductory clauses and phrases:

Because of problems we were having with the equipment, we postponed collecting the data.

To follow up on this lead, we tried changing phase ratios from $60:60$ to $45:55$, $50:50$, and $35:65$ to determine the right mix.

2. To set off parenthetical words and phrases:

Some of the materials were too light. *For example,* foam was inappropriate for the container. (The words *for example* are parenthetic.)

Particles are generated using a device similar to an ink jet; *however,* the device developed at the lab acts more like a pipette than an ink jet. (The word *however* is parenthetic.)

The maximum and time-weighted average concentrations, *as predicted by GENEEC,* are below all acute and chronic levels of concern. (The expression *as predicted by GENEEC* is parenthetic.)

The hydrophilic portion of the molecule remains in the polar solvent while the nonpolar portions, *which are hydrophobic,* are pushed into the air. (The expression *which are hydrophobic* is parenthetic.)

3. To separate three or more items in a series. The conjunction before the last item *(and, or, nor)* may be preceded by a comma (the serial comma). Most technical publications prefer the serial comma:

The instrument is equipped with lateral-centering electrodes, a homemade microscope, and a cooled CD camera.

4. To separate coordinate adjectives (adjectives that could logically be linked by *and*):

We added a large, crumpled piece of aluminum to the container.

In contrast, notice that you would not use a comma in an expression like *early warning system* because the word *early* explains *warning.*

A common error is to link independent clauses with a comma:

Load waste material into the autoclave, please do not overstuff the chamber.

To correct the sentence, either

· Place a period between the two independent clauses:

Load waste material into the autoclave. Please do not overstuff the chamber.

Or

· Link the two clauses with a semicolon:

Load waste material into the autoclave; please do not overstuff the chamber.

Ellipses

In text, use three points (. . .) to represent deleted material within a sentence:

Medewar comments that "a lecturer can be a bore . . . because he goes into quite unnecessary details about matters of technique."

Use four points for omissions at the end of a sentence.
Show changes in capitalization with brackets:

As Medewar comments, "[P]eople with anything to say can usually say it briefly."

Hyphens

What is the matter with these phrases?

long term storage stability
solvent free binder
a six day two week period
applications on an 11 to 16 day schedule
a time weighted average
water based neoprene

The answer is that they are all missing a necessary punctuation mark, the hyphen.

long-term storage stability
solvent-free binder
a six-day two-week period
applications on an 11- to 16-day schedule
a time-weighted average
water-based neoprene

Hyphens are a popular punctuation mark in technical text; you are likely to run into them at every turn, from *on-line documentation* to *menu-driven systems.*

Hyphens perplex students because they often appear between words in one example and then disappear in the next. For instance, you may see *on-line* on one page, but *online* on the next.

The reason is that hyphens are a very fluid, fast-changing part of English punctuation. Often when they are introduced in new compounds like *on-line*, they gradually disappear, and the two parts of the compound fuse: *online.* Many prefixes that used to be hyphenated, too, are vanishing. *Pre-test* has gone to *pretest*, *co-operation* to *cooperation.*

Some hyphens, though, remain, at least for now. There are two types of hyphens: soft hyphens and hard hyphens.

Soft hyphens are those inserted by the author to divide a word into two parts between the end of one line of text and the start of the next line. Avoid soft hyphens when possible, but if a division is unavoidable, break at the syllable, after the prefix, or before the suffix. Do not divide contractions, acronyms, abbreviations, or one-syllable words.

Hard hyphens are those used to separate the bases of a compound word *(work-station)* or to separate prefixes or suffixes from a base *(a cell-like configuration).* Use hard hyphens.

1. For numbers between 21 and 99 when written as words except for multiples of 10:

twenty-one, fifty-six

2. For fractions used within the narrative:

one-third of the container

3. For compounds beginning with a single capital letter:

O-rings

4. For coordinate compounds:

English-Chinese version

5. For premodifying expressions of age, weight, time, size, and quantity that are written open (no hyphen) when they are not pre-modifiers:

an apparatus that is five years old

but

a five-year-old apparatus

6. For ad hoc premodifying compounds:

a signal-to-noise ratio
a what-you-see-is-what-you-get system

7. For adjective compounds in which the second base is a partici-ple, an adjective, or a noun:

menu-driven
polynomial-based descrambler
a blue-gray mixture
a rock-hard substance
a high-frequency measurement

8. To separate a prefix or suffix from a base:
   • If the base begins with a capital or figure:

pre-1990

   • To avoid doubling an *i* or tripling a consonant:

anti-inflammatory, wall-like

   • To avoid ambiguity:

re-cover the container,

but

recover from a catastrophe

   • After *half, quasi,* and *self:*

half-finished

Don't use a hyphen if the first base in the compound ends in *ly:*

a poorly constructed apparatus

Parentheses and Brackets

Parentheses have an established place in technical prose, particularly for asides like table and figure citations and definitions of terms. Here are some of their common uses:

1. For figure and table citations:

Using this presumed alignment and other aspects associated with symmetry, it is possible to explain the anisotropy observed in the analyzed image (Figure 5).

2. To introduce abbreviations and acronyms:

An aerosol particle fluorescence microscope (APFM) is described for characterizing impurity chromophores within an aerosol particle.

3. For interpolations and asides, particularly of subsidiary information clarifying procedures or results:

By applying a voltage pulse to piezoelectric strips in the particle injector body, a small droplet (about 20-um radius) is squeezed from the orifice at the end of the tip.
It should be pointed out that no particular polarization state (i.e., x or y) is impressed on the surface by the incident radiation.

4. To enclose the numbers of items in lists that are run into text, rather than displayed. (In a displayed list, each item begins on a new line.):

These commands work (1) to reply to messages, (2) to forward messages to other addresses, and (3) to mark for deletion.

Use either brackets or parentheses for citations:

Several reports describe the value of magnetic resonance imaging (MRI) in visualizing the damage [1,3,7].

Microparticles in air, such as biological spores or other aerosol particles, partake in biological reproduction and the dissemination of disease, according to *Spread of Viral Infections of Aerosols* (1987; 17;89–131).

Use brackets

1. For interpolations within quotations. The brackets show the reader that the material within was added by the writer or editor, and was not spoken by the person quoted:

Feynmann comments in this context that "the phenomenon of colors produced by the *partial* reflection of white light by two surfaces is called iridescence [italics added]."

2. For parentheses within parentheses. For chemical and mathematical notation, use parentheses for the innermost item, followed by square brackets and then braces.

$$\langle I(\phi;\ \theta_m)\rangle \propto \mu^2 (a_{per})^2 \{[\cos(\theta_m)\sin(\phi)]^2$$
$$+\ (1/2)(a_{par}/a_{per})^2 [\sin(\theta_m)\cos(\phi)]^2\}$$

Semicolons

Semicolons are useful when you want to connect independent clauses tightly:

> The homogeneal light and rays which appear red, or rather make objects appear so, I call Rubrifick, or red-making; those which make objects appear yellow, green, blue, and violet, I call yellow-making, green-making, blue-making, violet-making, and so of the rest.
>
> *Isaac Newton*

A common error in writing is to link independent clauses with a comma:

> Solid samples are not homogeneous, a great deal of care has to be taken to melt the material completely.

If you want to join two independent clauses, you can, of course, use a coordinating conjunction *(and, but, for, or, nor, so, yet)*.

> Solid samples are not homogeneous, so a great deal of care has to be taken to melt the material completely.

A closer link is provided by the semicolon:

> Solid samples are not homogeneous; a great deal of care has to be taken to melt the material completely.

Use a semicolon to separate items in a list when the items themselves are punctuated:

> Members of the panel included Teresa Wong, representing Team 1, Georgetown, Washington, D.C.; George Sinclair, representing Team 2, Silver Spring, Maryland; and Herbert Singh, representing Team 3, Chevy Chase, Maryland.

Use a semicolon, not a comma, to link independent clauses joined by a conjunctive adverb *(however, therefore, thus, then, still, hence, indeed, instead, nonetheless, otherwise)*.
Not

> Solid samples are not homogeneous, therefore, a great deal of care has to be taken to melt the material completely.

But

> Solid samples are not homogeneous, therefore, a great deal of care has to be taken to melt the material completely.

Index